Deal Breakers

Deal Breakers

Breaking Out of Relationship Purgatory

Dr Bethany Marshall

SIMON &
SCHUSTER

London · New York · Sydney · Toronto

A CBS COMPANY

First published in Great Britain by Simon & Schuster UK Ltd, 2007
A CBS COMPANY

Originally published in the US in 2007 by
SIMON SPOTLIGHT ENTERTAINMENT,
An imprint of Simon & Schuster Children's Publishing
1230 Avenue of the Americas
New York, NY 10020

Designed by Yaffa Jaskoll

1 3 5 7 9 10 8 6 4 2

Simon & Schuster UK Ltd
Africa House
64–78 Kingsway
London WC2B 6AH

www.simonsays.co.uk

Simon & Schuster Australia
Sydney

A CIP catalogue record for this book
is available from the British Library.

ISBN-13: 978-1-8473-7061-7
ISBN-10: 1-8473-7061-6

Printed and Bound in Great Britain by
CPI Bath

For my wonderful husband, Mark, who inspired this book by offering a relationship where there is always a dialogue and never an impasse.

ACKNOWLEDGMENTS

I would like to thank my literary agent, Carrie Cook, a true go-getter, who approached me about writing this book and then made it happen.

To the rare and talented team at Simon Spotlight Entertainment, I am grateful for the opportunity to have cocreated this wonderful project with you.

Rick Richter, president of Simon & Schuster's Children's Publishing Division, thank you for your faith in *Deal Breakers*.

Patrick Price, my editor, who nurtured and developed this idea from the beginning—not only are you perceptive, poetic, and wise, but you helped me write a book that is both intellectually honest and entertaining.

Jen Bergstrom, Simon Spotlight Entertainment publisher, you are hip, savvy, and smart. Thank you for reading and rereading this manuscript and interjecting your invaluable advice.

Michael Nagin, your brilliant cover design captures the essence of *Deal Breakers*.

My thanks also to my publicists Jennifer Robinson and Sandi Mendelson, who helped give this book a voice.

I am especially grateful for my dear friend and colleague, Lucia Aparicio, LCSW. You are a brilliant diagnostician. Thank you for endless hours spent discussing and refining the concepts in this book.

To the instructors and training analysts at the Los Angeles Institute and Society for Psychoanalytic Studies, thank you for teaching me the value of making the unconscious conscious—for both my patients and my readers.

I am especially indebted to my precious husband, Mark. Thank you for making my manuscript better, for being a partner and a best friend, and for patiently reading countless Louis L'Amour novels while you waited for me to complete this book.

And finally, to my parents who have been married for forty-seven years, Dr. John and Gloria Marshall, thank you for surrounding me with the power of love and attachment.

CONTENTS

I am a psychoanalyst who helps women improve their relationships and their love lives. Over years of clinical practice, I have counseled countless women . . . and men . . . and couples from all walks of life.

When I listen to a woman who is facing a relationship challenge, I can usually tell in the first few minutes whether the problem is a deal breaker. And fairly soon, I am able to determine if she should work on it or walk away. How do I know? There are countless clues . . . for instance, whether or not her guy is motivated enough to make the changes that she needs . . . whether or not the problem is too serious to be fixed . . . and whether or not she is able to see the situation clearly.

And that is why I have written this book. I want *you* to know what *I* know about facing deal breakers and then determining what to do about them. And I want to help you achieve the healthy—and very possible—romance that you have dreamed of since you were a little girl. It *is* magical and wonderful to love a man who loves you in return—and in the way that you need. But it is a tragedy to commit your love and energy to the wrong man.

With this in mind, what is your deal breaker? A man who does not love you enough? A man who takes you out and talks only about himself? How about a man who doesn't talk at all? Or a man who is more interested in watching television and a local sports game instead of connecting to you?

What qualities make you instinctively cringe? If he's cheap? A liar? Emotionally detached? Jealous and possessive? What if he checks out other women while he's on a date with you?

Or maybe something less critical instinctively bugs you. He's a wonderful guy but uses random, weird phrases, like "foxy lady" and "hey, baby." Perhaps he has dirt under his fingernails. Or wears socks with his sandals. You do not want to appear shallow, but there's something deeper that is bothering you—you just can't put your finger on it yet.

Perhaps he seemed perfect in the beginning. But over time, he began to get on your nerves.

When character defects and attitudes bother you *this* much, it is because (whether you realize it or not) you are defining your breaking point—or rather, your *deal breaker*.

In the business world, a deal breaker is the one non-negotiable term that, if not agreed to, means the deal is off. But in the world of relationships, identifying your deal breaker can be much more promising, as it holds out the possibility of helping you understand where the relationship has gone wrong, what needs to be done in order to make it better, and when to walk away because, although you have done everything possible, it remains a no-win situation.

Women negotiate deals in their professional lives all the time. But why not in their personal relationships . . . especially when the stakes are potentially so much higher? (Granted, pulling out a contract over dinner might not be the best move, but it sure would make things a whole lot easier, wouldn't it?)

Instead, women often accept relationships in which they are constantly negotiating, yet never *defining* the terms of their deal. For instance, Linda, a twenty-four-year-old production assistant, came to my office with the worry that her boyfriend was taking advantage of her. They had lived together for one year and he had recently asked her to spend money redecorating their home. The tricky part was that he owned the house and had not yet made a marital commitment to her. Yet every time she asked him about the future, he would say, "Why do you keep questioning our relationship? If I didn't think you were marriage material, why would I be living with you?" So Linda sought therapy to resolve her growing doubtfulness and confusion about the relationship.

This was a deal breaker that anybody could spot a mile away! Her cheapskate boyfriend was asking for an emotional and financial investment from her, yet refusing to come clean about his own intentions (he had pulled the "Jedi" mind trick on her, making it seem like *she* had the problem). And Linda had become confused and forgotten that relationships—like business arrangements—are deals. Both parties have to agree to the terms. And if a nonnegotiable term is not agreed to, it is okay to walk away.

But because my misguided patient did not yet know about deal breakers, she succumbed to the same questions that women often ask in these types of situations:

"Am I making too big a deal out of this?"

"I wonder, is it him or is it me? I try to tell him how I feel, but he tells me that I am imagining things."

"Perhaps I should give him more time to make up his mind. I don't want to drive him away."

Miss Hoping for a Change missed the biggest deal breaker of all—*lack of a reciprocal emotional investment* (this common deal breaker will be discussed in an upcoming chapter). And instead, she tried to make the most of it and slumped deeper and deeper into a depression.

Once I helped Linda define her deal breaker, she was able to see that her boyfriend's lack of honesty was, in and of itself, a form of communication. She began to see things more clearly, and her confusion disappeared.

A deal breaker is a boundary that smart people set for themselves because they know that falling in love can make them do stupid things. The tricky thing about deal breakers, however, is that they are not always apparent at the beginning of a relationship. Romantic relationships require optimism, hope, and idealization to get off the ground. Because of this, important warning signs can easily be ignored.

A case in point is Carrie, a twenty-eight-year-old entertainment executive who got caught up in an exciting romance with a divorced man. Although he kept calling, he also kept telling her that he had lost most of his assets in his divorce and no longer believed in marriage. Carrie rationalized to herself that he was emotionally scarred and would eventually overcome his reservations about her. One day Carrie's lover left his briefcase open while taking a postsex shower. Carrie snooped and came across an old photograph of him and his ex-wife standing in front of a beautiful home, blissfully embracing each other. It was not until Carrie saw the picture that she was able to conceptualize what was wrong with the relationship. Namely, that she was dating a man who had once been willing to give himself to another woman but was now unwilling to share himself fully with her.

Of course, on some level Carrie had known this all along. But once she was able to define her deal breaker (in this case, that he wanted a fling rather than a commitment), she was able to define everything else that was wrong with the relationship. For instance, he frequently met her for sex (take-out) and rarely took her to dinner. He was secretive about important aspects of his life. And although they often talked late into the night, he never mentioned the future or told her that he cared about her.

Wrong, wrong, wrong! But the moment that Carrie defined her nonnegotiable term—that she wanted a relationship with a future—she liberated herself from everything else that was wrong with the relationship. Her relationship addiction was cured, and she felt free to engage in more rewarding romantic pursuits (please note that if her lover had been "The One," her deal breaker would have galvanized him to devote himself to her).

If you cannot effectively define the terms of your deal, then you will forever relegate yourself to relationship purgatory. Relationship purgatory, as the term implies, is neither heaven nor hell. It is merely a state in which the present is unfulfilling, and the future is the only thing that you can hope for. Relationship purgatory neither condemns you to extreme unhappiness nor liberates you into a joyful existence. It simply means that your future is always hanging in the balance.

Why would you want to live like that?

Why wouldn't you want to feel clear about your relationship? To know what the breaking points are, so that you can intelligently broach the subject of change before problems turn into a nuclear disaster? To know whether problems come from him or from you?

This book will help you observe problems as they occur and approach them in an intelligent and systematic manner.

For instance, Suzy brought her fiancé, Tom, to therapy because he kept criticizing her friends. Recently Tom had threatened to break off their engagement if she did not stop hanging out with them. In the first session Tom mentioned that he hated Suzy's friends because they were wild and she became a different person around them. When I inquired further, he expressed fear that Suzy would become as "out of control" as them. Within a few minutes it became clear that Tom feared he could not trust Suzy unless she was under his firm control. And because they were about to get married, her freewheeling behavior made him worry that she would not be a loyal wife and good mother. I made the comment to Tom, "Perhaps you can't trust what you can't control." It soon became clear that Tom's fears—not Suzy's behavior— were out of control. Once the problem was defined, the true work on the relationship began. Tom began to understand that Suzy's ability to have fun was what drew him to her in the first place. With help, he was able to see her spontaneity for what it was rather than what he feared it would turn into. Suzy could see that Tom's insecurities, if left unchecked, could turn into a deal breaker. And her clarity helped her gauge whether or not he was making the progress that she needed. Their relationship improved because Tom was willing to control his insecurities instead of controlling her (before coming to therapy he was experiencing more ups and downs than a shopping mall elevator the day after Thanksgiving).

I am going to introduce for you a new and empowering definition of a deal breaker: *A deal breaker is a negative or standstill arrangement that, once recognized, can be used as a tool for positive change.* Once you learn to negotiate deal breakers in your love life, you will come into a position of true personal power and create the happiness you deserve.

What's Your Deal? CHAPTER 1

What do you absolutely want out of your relationship? Do you know?

You may consider yourself wise, self-sufficient, and a good judge of character. Your girlfriend's troubled love life always seems transparent and filled with unnecessary drama. But when faced with your *own* murky relationship waters, the easy answers seem to disappear.

Perhaps it is easy to analyze your girlfriend's relationship because what constitutes a deal breaker for her may not necessarily constitute a deal breaker for you. Conversely, a romantic situation that seems like nirvana to you might feel like sheer hell for her.

So how can you judge a true deal breaker?

A deal breaker is a character flaw or emotional stance that significantly deteriorates the quality of a relationship. Note: Deal breakers are *not* minor annoying habits such as your boyfriend's chewing with his mouth open or your husband's endlessly quoting sports statistics. Rather, they are qualities that erode your most cherished aspirations for a satisfying love relationship.

But in order to spot a deal breaker, you must first have a deal. By this, I mean that you must know what you hope to get out of a relationship (other than two carats in a platinum setting). Knowing what you want is important because all relationships are built upon arrangements. Some are financial arrangements. Some are emotional arrangements. Some are marital arrangements. Some are sexual arrangements. Your relationship may contain some, or all, aspects of the arrangements just mentioned. Arrangements are best when they are agreed upon by both parties and flexibly negotiated over time.

But what if you don't know what you want? Or you settle for an arrangement that makes you unhappy? Or you grew up in a household where nothing was discussed or explored, so you never learned to ask for what you wanted?

[Nicky's story]

Nicky, a twenty-two-year-old graduate student, came to therapy because she felt anxious about her "dating" relationship.

I put "dating" in quotes because Nicky revealed to me that her relationship consisted primarily of watching late-night TV together, cuddling until four in the morning, and then having sex. After these nights of so-called passion, her boyfriend would disappear and forget to call her for several days.

This was not a dating relationship. This was a booty call! But Nicky was young and naive, and had not yet articulated to herself what she wanted out of a relationship. Thus, she could not spot a deal breaker even though it was staring her straight in the face.

I broached the subject of deal breakers by educating Nicky about normal dating relationships; namely, that a man's willingness to call in advance and take a woman to dinner is an indicator of his willingness to invest his emotions in her. Nicky's newfound knowledge helped her realize that she was in a sexual arrangement, not a dating arrangement. Once she acknowledged that she wanted a boyfriend instead of a sex buddy, she realized that his lack of emotional investment was a deal breaker. She told him that she wanted an exclusive dating relationship that involved dinners out and time spent with mutual friends, but she could tell by his reluctance that he was not "The One."

If you think back to the last time you were unhappy in a relationship, there is a great likelihood that your partner was doing something that undermined the arrangement you were hoping for. For example, if your boyfriend consistently refused to attend family holidays, then he was probably ruining your hopes of a relationship arrangement that included interest in each other's life and a possible future together. If he continually questioned your decisions, he could have been undermining your dreams of a relationship built upon trust. If he flew into irrational jealous rages, then he was possibly dashing your hopes of being in a stable relationship arrangement.

A deal breaker is not a deal breaker unless it destroys something that is precious to you.

But deal breakers are emotional, so they're easy to miss. They're feelings, so there's nothing to sign. And they can be difficult to talk about, because they're typically unspoken.

Here are some important aspects of common relationship arrangements and the deal breakers that can destroy them:

You need autonomy.	He wants to oversee and approve your friendships and date book.
You are ambitious.	Not only has he been in the same job for fifteen years, but his uniform still includes a paper hat.

You need a relationship where conflicts are discussed and resolved.	To him, resolving conflicts means getting you to put a sock in it.
You want to feel special.	He is withholding and cheap.
You need consistency. You want to know that when you see him, he is the same person he was the last time you saw him.	He is so moody that you are convinced he has PMS.
You like the idea of monogamy.	He's faithful, but when he sees another woman his tongue unfurls like a cartoon rodent's.

And so it is with deal breakers. One person has a need. The other will not fulfill it. One person wants to get married. The other person does not. One person wants fidelity. The other does not. One person wants freedom. The other is only interested in control.

Deal breakers undermine the very conditions that make it possible to love. And as such, they constitute a warning that the relationship needs either to dissolve or to change. Unfortunately, you may not know what you want out of a relationship. Or if you do, you may feel guilty about creating the situation that works best for you. Thus, you may remain unaware of the factors that make a relationship impossible. But do not be discouraged. Being in a good relationship is not rocket science. By the time you are finished with this book, you will know *exactly* what you want.

In the meantime, here's a little tidbit to think about. Regardless of the arrangement that you are trying to build for yourself, your healthy relationship should include three important ingredients:

1. Reciprocity

Both of you are equally invested in the relationship.

2. Generativity

The relationship generates something new (a new experience, a new understanding, a new solution) with each encounter—thus it is always moving forward.

3. Honesty

You feel free to tell him what's on your mind and he responds by revealing his true thoughts, motivations, and intentions. Thus, you continually get to know each other better.

It's a red flag if you have to call your friends or obtain a PhD to decipher what he is trying to communicate to you.

For example, you think that you are having a discussion, but you walk away from each conversation feeling confused. Or you worry about whether he's coming clean or telling you the truth. Or you try to communicate with him, but he hears something other than what you said. And you begin to realize that if you cannot communicate about the simplest of things, you might not be able to build a good relationship arrangement together.

(THE SIGN)

Is there one relationship problem that eats away at you, but you don't know why? You keep trying to connect the dots, but you can't—and you wonder if there's a deeper issue that you are missing? Or whether the problem is serious enough to be considered a deal breaker?

The answer: A deal breaker is not a one-time fight. Nor is it an excuse to put distance between you and him. *A deal breaker is a sign of everything else that is wrong in a relationship.*

Sometimes, deal breakers erupt into consciousness during one awful moment (like discovering a pile of bounced checks when you have long suspected that he is irresponsible). Or they are characterized by a series of seemingly minor events that add up to one big problem (like many social events during which he inappropriately brags—worse yet, about his baseball card collection). Often deal breakers surface in social contexts, where it becomes easier to view your partner through the eyes of others you trust.

For instance, Jim entered therapy to understand his inability to assert himself. Although Jim is a brilliant oncologist, he has a poorly defined sense of self. Thus, he is constantly seeking approval and is rarely willing to say what he thinks. In a recent session, Jim described a painful breakup that occurred in his early twenties. He had been dating a girl who overlooked many instances in which Jim had exaggerated his accomplishments in order to gain approval. About one year into the relationship, she introduced Jim to her parents. During the introduction, Jim lied and told them he was a licensed MD when in fact he had not yet attended medical school. His girlfriend became worried and broke off the relationship.

As I listened to Jim's painful recollection, I thought, *Of course she broke up with you! This was a deal breaker! The poor girl had probably been listening to your thinly veiled lies and exaggerations for months. But when she observed you lying to her parents, and was able to view the problem from their perspective, she was finally able to conceptualize everything else that was wrong with the relationship.*

Women who come to me for help initially express surface complaints about the men in their lives:

"For some reason, I hate the way he dresses."

"I don't know why, but I only have road rage when he's in the passenger seat."

"He tells me that he won't spend an entire weekend together. Is it wrong for me to feel upset?"

"He tells me that I am shallow and immature. That really bothers me. Should it?"

"When we have sex, he fixates on my breasts and ignores the rest of me. It hurts my feelings, and I'm not sure why."

When I hear complaints such as these, I usually ask, "What does his unwillingness to spend an entire weekend together mean to you?" or "Does it remind you of anything else that is wrong with the relationship?" I ask these questions because seemingly trivial complaints are often a sign of something much larger. And often, the woman's original concern is backed up by other observations and worries that reflect the true significance of the original complaint. For instance, the man who fixated on his girlfriend's breasts had other parallel problems (if he hadn't, it would not have been a deal breaker . . . just creepy and annoying). He only related to the parts of her that felt exciting and pleasurable to him and ignored the rest (he forgot that breasts are typically attached to a person). Therefore, he could not understand anything about her that did not relate directly to himself. This major problem had an impact on the rest of his relationships, as he saw people as objects to meet his needs rather than as individuals with thoughts, feelings, and desires of their own.

Whenever I explore a woman's relationship complaints, I can tell if they constitute a deal breaker. If she's referring to a deal breaker, her original complaint will be related to many other problems in the relationship. If she's trying to work through a curable problem, then her worries will either have to do with her own history (for example, she was abandoned as a child and is now anxious whenever her husband goes out of town) or the problem can easily be fixed.

True deal breakers are symptomatic of underlying relationship problems. They point to something severe, such as a relationship impasse or a destructive emotional issue that cannot be resolved. As such, deal breakers become signposts of other dynamics that are unworkable in a relationship.

[Giselle's story]

Giselle came to therapy to talk about her relationship with her boyfriend. In the second session, she told me that her boyfriend wanted to take back a diamond tennis bracelet that he had given her for Christmas. His plan was to exchange it for an engagement ring that Giselle had admired.

On the face of it, the infraction seemed benign. I mean, she had admired an engagement ring that he now wanted to buy for her! As the story unfolded, however, I learned that Giselle's lover frequently bought her gifts after closing business deals. But the minute they had a minor quarrel, he would retaliate by retrieving her gifts and returning them for cash. His problem was compounded by a belief that Giselle was a money-grubbing girl who only wanted him for his money. (He screwed people out of money for a living. He assumed Giselle did too.)

Of course, the gift-returning scenario merely reflected layers of other relationship problems. He frequently took things personally and would become upset at minor infractions. He was constantly breaking up with Giselle and then reuniting with her. The breakups seemed to occur during periods when he was feeling his oats and wanted to go out for a good time with his friends. As with the gifts, he was constantly offering his love and then taking it back.

Once Giselle understood that *she* was like the bracelet—easily bought and easily returned—she was able to use the realization that this was a deal breaker to implement important changes in her life.

Note: Once Giselle realized that the gift-returning incidents were symptomatic of deeper relationship problems, she wasalso able to understand that the relationship arrangement was not working for her. Although she wanted a relationship that potentially included marriage, her lover was too busy breaking off the relationship to create a secure future for them.

*   *   *

Because deal breakers are signs of other relationship problems, they can slap you in the face while other important problems are hidden from view. For instance, if you are in a difficult relationship, you may find that there is one annoying habit that drives you crazy. Or one big problem that seems to eclipse everything else. The problem could be parenting skills, control, arguing, lack of money, ambiguity, indecisiveness, et cetera. But if the horrible problem is a deal breaker, it will be a reflection of other problems that are equally important.

Perhaps your one big complaint is the only tangible sign that other things are wrong. For instance, you focus on your man's alcoholism when underlying selfishness is the true problem (alcoholism can be fixed by a twelve-step program, but selfishness might not). Or you are upset that your boyfriend won't get married, when his lack of emotional interest is the real issue.

Once you notice a deal breaker, you can't unsee it. You can pretend you didn't see it, like the man who pretends no one notices his sideways, back-of-the-head comb-over, but anyone who cares about *you* will see it.

Deal breakers can be helpful, in that they can help you picture other relationship problems. For instance, I once treated the girlfriend of a wealthy real estate developer. This thirty-six-year-old woman had put ten years of her life on hold, and would often fly to various parts of the world to meet him (so many times that she had accumulated enough frequent flyer miles to orbit the moon). At the end of each visit he would hand her five thousand dollars in cash, which she was supposed to live on until the next time. She chose not to get a job or develop a career, because she believed that her availability would secure her future with him. (After all, beauty duty is a full-time job.) But as you probably guessed, if he wanted to marry her, he would have already done it.

One day my patient picked up a city magazine, and guess who was there on the cover? Her boyfriend. The caption read "Mr. So-and-So Donates $50 Million to Build a Museum Wing in His Name."

She was devastated. But when she read the caption, she was able to envision everything else that was wrong with the relationship. Namely, that he was more devoted to outside interests than to her. That she had not accurately defined her relationship arrangement (she thought it was an emotional arrangement, when in fact it was merely a sexual arrangement). And she acted as though she were his fiancée, when in fact she was merely a playmate. These realizations led her to the conclusion that the relationship was financially disadvantageous and emotionally unfair. That she had sold her soul for an illusion. And most important, that her lover did not care about her (the biggest deal breaker of all).

Once she broached the subject of his self-involvement,

he responded by reminding her that she was not obligated to be in a relationship with him. Her confusion cleared and she broke off the relationship.

If a problem is not representative of deeper issues, it may not be a deal breaker. For instance, giving you herpes is not necessarily a deal breaker. Not announcing he was about to is. Remember: A deal breaker is only a deal breaker if it is symptomatic of other destructive relationship dynamics.

Thus, if your husband slept with another woman on a business trip yet has always been an excellent and loyal partner, it may not be a deal breaker! (Though it is common to view sexual infidelity as symptomatic of other relationship problems, this is not always the case. Not to undermine the sting of betrayal, but I have seen more couples successfully negotiate sexual infidelity than a lack of mutual interest or relationship craziness.) If he loses his job and becomes temporarily financially dependent—yet has always been responsible—then it may not be a deal breaker.

So here's the tricky point: When is it a deal breaker, and when is it not?

It is a deal breaker when it is the tip of the misery iceberg and you know that there is more lurking beneath the surface. Or when it destroys the relationship arrangement you need in order to feel fulfilled and happy.

It is not a deal breaker when it is merely one bad thing that has happened, and is not related to other fundamental problems in the relationship.

It's About Time

Now you know what a deal breaker is—a negative or standstill arrangement that stands in the way of happiness. And it points to other, deeper issues that are troubling you. But are you willing to spot and accept it?

Or do you catch yourself stubbornly making excuses for bad behavior? You recognize a problem, but you hope that it will magically go away or somehow cure itself through the passage of time?

Or you find yourself hoping for future changes that will compensate for that which is missing in the present, rationalizing that the solution is right around the corner?

You say to yourself:

"If he gave me a ring, I would feel better about him . . . or at least I wouldn't feel any worse."

"If we stopped fighting, this would be the perfect relationship."

"If I could convince him to go to therapy, maybe he would change and his mood swings would go away."

"I'm sure that when he gets to know me better, he will be more available."

"He just needs to learn to trust me."

One thing that all these statements have in common is an irrational perception that a future event will solve a present problem. Let me state this clearly: There is no magic future. And there is no magic moment. Only one thing is magical: the present. *Because deal breakers occur in real time.* They are being acted out in the present, and therefore they should be solved in the present.

Worrying about the future will only derail you from clearly comprehending the present. And passively hoping for a change will cost you months and years of your life. Why? Well, what do *you* think? What makes you think that if he doesn't want to quit smoking pot and sitting aimlessly around the house now, he will be more likely to give it up next year? Or that if he is insanely jealous, he will magically come to his senses in a few months? The same thing is true for discussions. Have you had one lately? If he can't have one now, don't lose sleep hoping for a little heart-to-heart next weekend.

Problems that are not resolved today will most likely never be resolved. It hurts to hear, but it's the truth.

[Eva's story]

When Eva arrived at her first therapy session, she had been driving around with divorce papers in the trunk of her car for eight months. Although she had consulted with an attorney, she was simply too afraid to proceed with the divorce and have her husband served.

After ten months of treatment, Eva finally sought the separation she so desperately wanted. She had been the sole income earner for fifteen years while her husband stayed at home working on screenplays. For fifteen years, day and night, he would park himself in the living room, bark out orders, intimidate the children, dominate the household, and insist upon peace and quiet. And yet, he never sold a screenplay. Nor did he generate anything of value for Eva and their children (like most narcissists, he expected reward without appropriate achievement). Meanwhile, Eva obediently earned a living, cooked meals, took the kids to their games, et cetera, et cetera.

As soon as Eva asked for a divorce, her husband got a job, made money, lost weight, asked women on dates, and created the life that Eva had so desperately wanted.

When it was all over, I commented to Eva, "Don't you think it is odd that you supported him for so many years while he tinkered with screenplays, yet the moment you filed for divorce he became self-supporting?" Eva wearily answered, "When he told me he was working as hard as he could, I believed him. I guess I kept thinking that things would change."

Had Eva seen her deal breaker as a real-time occurrence, she would have given her dependent husband the boot before she lost her youth and her sanity. She would have comprehended that her husband did not want to change, and she would have begun to realize that their arrangement was not working for her. Eva needed a partner who would willingly generate financial resources for their family; however, her husband had not wanted to.

In therapy, Eva began to realize that her husband's unwillingness to work was symptomatic of other, deeper problems. For instance, her husband felt entitled to be supported without effort on his own part. Thus, he was a big fat baby with no mature motivation of his own.

So do I need to make it clearer? If he doesn't want to change now, he never will. And if he *is* capable of changing, waiting for tomorrow robs you of your dreams for today.

(WHAT'S GOOD FOR HIM IS GOOD FOR YOU)

You are beginning to define your deal breaker and you know that time is slipping away. But how do you broach the subject of your discontent? What are you supposed to say?

Deal breakers are tools for promoting change, not weapons to wield against another person who does not meet your needs. And deal breakers provide a powerful opportunity for dialogue. But you have to negotiate your deal fairly, or you may not get what you want. If you coerce him, he'll either pretend to agree or break up with you. If *you* give in to *him*, you will be unhappy. If you can learn to appropriately assert yourself, however, you will discover whether he cares and whether he's the right guy for you.

What is self-assertion? It is stating your needs and giving him a chance to respond. If he doesn't respond, you can leave. Remember, it is just a relationship. Attendance is optional!

Here is an example of self-assertion:

"I've been thinking about your constant fear that I will cheat on you. Because I am one hundred percent committed, and have never given you reason to fear, I have come to the conclusion that your jealousy is irrational and bullying. Please stop. If you can't, you must get help. If you do not change, I may have to rethink our relationship or seek a better quality of life."

Self-assertion has several important components:

1. Revealing your feelings, preferences, and needs.

2. Giving him a chance to respond.

3. Willingness to walk away if he does not make an effort.

Revealing your feelings, preferences, and needs is critical (think of this as "Relationship 101"). You may be tempted to hide your feelings for fear of criticism and/or abandonment. How unfair! If you do not reveal yourself, your partner will never have a chance to respond. And giving him a chance to respond is what makes the negotiation fair. Besides, if you already know that he's unwilling to respond, then why are you in this relationship (and why don't you skip ahead to Chapter 13, "Breaking the Deal")?

If your partner decides not to make the changes you have requested, then you know where he stands and can allow him to have the life that he wants (even if that means that you might not be in the picture). And although that might be disappointing, what is good for him *is* good for you. If he cannot respond to your suffering, it is better for you to separate.

If you cannot assert your needs, you'll either give up or play games to get even. And if you cannot clearly articulate your position, you may resort to shaming and humiliating him. In either case, you are failing to check in with him and hear his side of the story, denying him a fair chance to respond, and missing out on the opportunity to determine if he really wants to change.

[Smith's story]

Smith came to therapy to deal with a messy divorce. He was married to a powerful woman who raised their only child while Smith worked diligently in the family business. Although they had occasionally experienced financial difficulty, Smith worked hard so that his wife could stay at home. As the divorce proceedings began, Smith's business began to deteriorate. His wife became angry, realizing that she might have to return to work.

In a recent session, Smith revealed the following: "I guess I should have paid better attention at the beginning of the relationship. When Jessica told me that she wanted a child, I knew that I did not. And when she told me that she wanted to stay at home instead of going to work, I knew that I would have a difficult time supporting her. I tried to tell her, but she was bent on getting her way. And I was terrified that she would leave, so I gave in. Perhaps if she had not been so militant in negotiating for what she wanted, I could have been more honest. I *did* know what I wanted—but I was just too scared to be more forthright."

Although Jessica appeared to be self-assertive, she had not listened carefully to Smith's feelings, nor had she given him a chance to honestly respond. Thus, she made an arrangement that worked only for her and ultimately doomed herself to a life of raising her son alone.

For every story there is an equal and opposite story. In other words, the man who does not respond and/or does not change is in fact sending a message—*that his choices are working for him*. And the deal breaker that makes you unhappy may, in fact, be serving a purpose in his life. For instance, the man who refuses to marry may know that he is not the man for you. And the emotional baby who cannot grow up may be doing the best that he can—yet still be an inferior partner. On the other hand, the man who willingly adapts to your needs as you adapt to his is the best candidate for a long-term happy alliance.

Therefore, relationship problems should always be discussed. And discussions should never be coercive or threatening. Remember: A power tool effectively gets you what you want. A weapon is only fit for war.

(DEAL BREAKER CHEAT SHEET)

You've now educated yourself about deal breakers. But you may still be asking yourself, "Now what do I do? How do I spot a convincing deal breaker?" Here is a little guide in case you are still unclear.

Characteristics of a deal breaker:

• You work harder than he does to fix his problems or make the relationship better.

• You keep asking yourself, "Is it him or is it me?"

- You hope that he will magically become better at some point in the future (for instance, that he will become sober, stop controlling you, become more affectionate, achieve more, et cetera). And you recognize that if he doesn't, you will be intolerably unhappy.

- You constantly worry about how the relationship is going to affect your future.

- You continually suppress your personality in order to avoid conflicts.

- You feel mistrusted to such a great degree that you are frightened to have outside friends or influences.

- He feels that you are either "for him" or "against him." When he is in a good emotional place, he believes that you are on his side. When he is in a bad emotional place, he feels that you are against him and do not have his best interests at stake.

- You, and only you, are unhappy.

- You long to make a connection with him but are unable to do so.

- You care more about him than he seemingly does about you.

• He consistently draws his own conclusions without listening to what you are saying. Thus, you are a product of his fantasies and he is incapable of recognizing you as an individual with thoughts, feelings, and motivations of your own.

• He lacks empathy or remorse and is unconcerned about how you feel.

• You meet his needs, but he seldom meets yours.

• Problems are never resolved, and nothing is ever gained.

(COMMONLY ASKED QUESTIONS ABOUT DEAL BREAKERS)

QUESTION: Can a deal breaker occur at any time during a relationship? I mean, what if I am married to a man for twenty years and he has an affair or becomes an alcoholic?
ANSWER: Although a deal breaker might occur at any time, it is unlikely that it will appear from out of the blue. Remember, deal breakers are symptomatic of other problems in a relationship. Therefore, they rarely surface late in the game.

QUESTION: What if I talk to him about a deal breaker and he does not respond?

ANSWER: Lack of a response is, in and of itself, a form of communication. If he does not respond, then perhaps he cannot self-reflect, cannot cope with relationship realities, cannot seek solutions, or cannot empathetically respond to you. In other words, he simply cannot—or will not—change.

QUESTION: If the deal breaker does not get better, do I have to leave the relationship?
ANSWER: No. But you better stock up on Prozac and Dove bars, because you *will* become depressed.

QUESTION: Even if he does not want to change now, is it possible that he might want to work on the deal breaker at some point in the future?
ANSWER: No. People do what they want to do, and they don't do what they don't want to do. If he wanted to change, he would either be in an ongoing process of seeking solutions (going to AA, making a good-faith effort, seeking therapy, engaging in dialogue with you), or he would have fixed the problem by now.

QUESTION: I have a relationship problem that is a big deal breaker. But we have two small children. Shouldn't we stay together for them?
ANSWER: What children need most are two parents who love each other and who model what it is like to be in a healthy

relationship. Sounds like you need to get cracking, or they will grow up and find unhealthy relationships of their own. And is that what you really want for your children?

QUESTION: I know that his personality problem is a deal breaker, but I am afraid that if I leave, he will fall apart.
ANSWER: You are so busy gluing him together that you are forgetting the most important deal of all: Your life is your own and only you can live it.

Although it may feel difficult to define the relationship issues that make you unhappy, it is not an insurmountable endeavor. And though it may feel like a potential catastrophe to express your needs to your partner and see if he can respond, it is not. It *is* a high-stakes risk—but one that's necessary to secure true happiness.

Women who come to my office with a broken heart and shattered dreams invariably confess that the problem in their relationship was readily apparent. But the fear of loss, the thrill of the chase, and the determination to turn him around overrode common sense and the realization that they were on the fast boat to nowhere.

Once they defined and confronted their deal breaker, however, they found the happiness they had been chasing. And they began to build the life they had been seeking all along.

Do You See What I See?

CHAPTER 3

I'm going to hand you the best tool you'll ever have. It is what I use when helping couples who want to help themselves.

The tool? The knowledge that most difficult men fall into five personality types: The Scriptwriter, The Man in Charge, The Man Without Fault, The Invisible Man, and The Little Boy Who Poses as a Man. Once you understand these types, you will know what you are getting into before you become emotionally attached, and free yourself to begin relationships without the fear of repeating bad experiences.

If you have been together for some time, deciphering his personality type will help you answer the questions, "Who is this man? Is he capable of changing? How do I talk to him about the problems that are affecting us?"

Comprehending these five personalities will assist you in pinpointing underlying conflicts that are surfacing in your relationship and develop a strategy for talking about them. Once you understand his personality, you will gain a clearer picture of who he is and why the two of you are experiencing problems. You will then be able to educate instead of berate, and communicate instead of fixate.

People do not always fall into neat categories; thus, more than one personality type may apply to your man. The more serious the problem, the more deal breaker categories he will fall into. The less serious the problem, the easier it will be for both of you to talk about it and thus initiate change.

[Meredith's story]

When Peter first met Meredith, he was enamored of her. But over time, he began to pick her apart. When she threw a cocktail party for her friends, he criticized the wine. When she met him for breakfast on a Saturday, he commented that she looked like a ghost without makeup. And when she wore a French maid's outfit to a Halloween party, he mentioned that her thighs looked dimply (yes, Peter is an idiot).

In therapy, I educated Meredith about Peter's personality. I let her know that at the core of his personality was a wish to devalue and criticize others in order to reinforce his own overestimation of himself. Upon learning this, she began to hear his criticisms in a whole new light. Instead of feeling small, she began to observe that Peter was diminishing her. She stopped trying too hard and instead began to hold him accountable for his mistreatment.

Once she helped Peter view the problem from her perspective, and once he gained a better understanding of his issues, he was able to work on himself instead of taking his personality problems out on her (in the end, though, he was still an idiot).

If you want to work on your relationship, you must help your partner see himself though your eyes. Can he see the same things in himself that you see in him? Based upon his personality type, do you understand what he sees in you? If he does not see you accurately, can you correct his misunderstandings?

If you can work on these issues, then you are halfway through fixing deal-breaking problems in your relationship. The concept of a deal breaker is illuminating, as it informs you about where the relationship has gone wrong and what you need to do in order to make it better. If you can help him see what you see, attempt to understand the situation from his perspective, and encourage him to respond, then the relationship will become more fluid and you will be able to craft an arrangement that works for both of you.

Embedded in the next five chapters are the most

common (but not all) deal breakers. And at the end of each chapter is a section that outlines common deal breaker scenarios, when to work on them, and when to walk away. Once you understand the dynamics of his personality and of your relationship, have reviewed the potential deal breaker scenarios, and have read the remaining chapters that teach you how to negotiate for what you want, you will be fully prepared to spot and handle any and all deal breaker situations that may come your way.

The Scriptwriter

CHAPTER 4

*The Scriptwriter decides who you are without consulting you. He embraces
the belief "I know you better than you know yourself."*

Does your boyfriend or husband understand you? When you
share your thoughts, does he know what you are saying?
When you bare your soul, does he get it? Or does everything get convoluted and twisted, and by the time you are
finished explaining yourself, you have a big, nasty fight on
your hands?

If he makes up his own mind about you regardless of what
you say and do, perhaps he is a Scriptwriter. The Scriptwriter
will try to cast you into a role without regard for your true
personality. He may even imagine that he knows you better
than you know yourself.

(FIRST IMPRESSIONS)

When you first meet a Scriptwriter, he may render a judgment that has nothing to do with you. For instance, he may say, "You are quite opinionated," when you are merely expressing yourself. Or he may feel that he owns you, when you've only just met. The tricky thing about The Scriptwriter is that he picks up on small details about you in order to support his false impressions. Therefore, it can be difficult to wiggle out of a role once he has cast you in it.

When you spend a great deal of time with a Scriptwriter, you may feel coerced into expressing thoughts and feelings that are not truly your own. Although you may realize that you are fueling his fantasies, you may rationalize to yourself that eventually he will understand you. But over time, you begin to realize that he is unable to recognize your uniqueness.

(WARNING SIGNS)

Because The Scriptwriter draws his own conclusions without developing a deep understanding of what you are saying, you may feel that he is talking to his idea of you rather than to who you are. As if he's making love to a fantasy rather than real flesh and blood—that you are his creation or an extension of what is going on in his mind.

For instance, if you're having sex with him and move ever so slightly, he may say, "Oh, you're a wild one" (even if you were merely trying for a better position). If you return his call, he may say, "Oh, you're hunting me down" (even though he was the one who called you first). If you lightly flirt with him, he might say, "I know what you have at home in your closet! A pair of thigh-high patent leather boots, a whip, chains, and a pair of handcuffs" (even though he doesn't know you and has never seen your wardrobe).

The Scriptwriter will try to interpret everything through one lens. If he is afraid of being controlled, he might experience you as a dominatrix. If he is afraid of being bled dry, he might experience you as a black widow. And if he is afraid of being betrayed, he might forever experience you as the woman who is about to skip out on him. On the other hand, if he needs to feel that you will never be unfaithful or dirtied, he may view you as a virgin or a Madonna (not her—the real one). And if he needs to feel important, he may put you on a pedestal so that he can feel important too. Once he captures you in a certain light, his perception may become ingrained and difficult to change.

The more you struggle to redefine your role in relation to this man, the more you could feel entrapped. For instance, let's say he casts you in the role of cheater and you program a special ring tone into your phone so that you can answer his calls and reassure him that you are not cheating. As soon as you get called into a meeting at work and are unable to answer his call, he may become suspicious and insist that there is no good reason that you were not available. Because you have begun to act out the role of rehabilitated-cheater-who-proves-that-she's-not-really-lying, you have unwittingly reinforced his script. The more you struggle, the more the noose will be tightened. And the more you explain yourself, the more he could believe that you are trying to throw him off track. He has projected his ideas into you, and you are acting them out.

How did The Scriptwriter come to be this way? Once you get to know him, you learn that this is how his care-takers treated him. For example, perhaps his mother did not see him for who he is. Instead, he was a character in a script that *she* wrote for *him*. Or a participant in her personal drama. And because she did not see him accurately, he is now unable to see you accurately.

[Amanda's story]

Amanda and Sam were introduced to each other at the company picnic and began dating soon thereafter. Although they both worked as sales executives at the same corporation, they had never run into each other before. Almost immediately Sam began to treat Amanda as if she were a subordinate.

He would help her map out her sales calls and organize her expense reports. Eventually he began to claim responsibility for her professional accomplishments. When Amanda received a sizable merit bonus, Sam recommended that she spend it on a joint vacation since he had been "instrumental in her career." And because Amanda had acted out his script and accepted his help, she felt she had no choice but to share her bonus. So she turned over the money and continued to accept his advice. Within two years Sam became convinced that Amanda could not pick out a parking space without his help.

The inappropriateness of the role in which she had been cast did not become apparent to Amanda until she invited Sam to meet her family. During dinner Sam bragged to them about how he had boosted Amanda's job performance. After dinner Amanda's sister pulled her aside and said, "I don't understand. He acts like you were nothing until he came along. But you put yourself through college, launched your own career, bought your own house, and even purchased a car that is better than his. What's happening here? Have you lost your mind?"

In a flash, Amanda realized that she had become a character in a play that was written and produced by Sam. He *thought* she was incapable, so she *acted* incapable. He thought he was responsible for her success, so she stood by and gave him all the credit. It was not until she realized that Sam had a distorted view of her that she began to fully comprehend her folly.

*   *   *

Sam was convinced that Amanda could not function adequately without him—even though *he* was the one who was desperate for *her* recognition and reassurance. In fact, women who live with Scriptwriters will notice many curious reversals. For instance, The Scriptwriter may fear that you are needy even though he is the one who will not let go. Or he may accuse you of neglecting him, when he is the one who does not want to make a commitment. He might accuse you of obsessing about marriage, when he is the one who constantly worries about walking down the aisle. Or he might experience you as being all about the money, although he is constantly preoccupied with finances.

Why does he do this? The Scriptwriter was raised by parents who unconsciously displaced their own feelings onto him. For instance, when his mother was hungry, she imagined that he was hungry and then fed him. And when she felt angry, she projected her anger onto him and imagined that he was angry too. Sometimes she even imagined that he was angry at her, when she was angry at him. And because she could not distinguish her feelings from his feelings, he did not learn to distinguish what was happening inside of him from what other people were feeling.

The Scriptwriter's confusion can be so profound that he causes you to act out and exemplify his own hopes and fears. For instance, when Melanie met Jack, he told her that his last wife had taken him to the cleaners. Because Melanie did not want to look like a money-grubbing gold digger, she made sure that she paid for half of their dates. Unbeknownst to her, however, she was already acting out the "you-are-going-to-eventually-take-me-for-all-I'm-worth" script by proving to him that she was unlike the others (thus indulging his fear by reacting to it). Desperate to climb out of the role in which she had been cast, Melanie signed a prenup prior to marrying Jack. And when the marriage dissolved ten years later, she walked away with only the clothes on her back. Looking back, the irony of the reversal struck her. Although Jack had been terrified of being financially taken advantage of, it was he who had taken advantage of her.

The only way to fix The Scriptwriter is to refuse to conform to his script (rewrites make him crazy). For instance, Amanda should have refused Sam's advice and kept her merit bonus for herself. And Melanie should have let Jack pay for some of their dates. After all, what is the worst thing that could have happened? That Sam and Jack could have become suspicious and refused to continue the relationship? What would have been so bad about that? Wasn't it worse for them to continue in a relationship with someone who didn't understand them?

(HOW TO KNOW IF HE'S A SCRIPTWRITER)

One of the best ways to know if he's a Scriptwriter is to listen to what he tells you on the first date. For example, if he tells you that his last girlfriend lied and that he doesn't trust women, he is already writing your script. And if he tells you that his last girlfriend lied, but that he *knows* that *you* are not like *her,* he's also writing a script. If he can only draw inferences based upon past relationships or upon whom he imagines you to be, then the curtain has lifted and the play has begun. If, however, he tells you that his last girlfriend lied to him, and he was surprised because he generally likes women and has had good relationship experiences, then the sky is the limit, because he is open to the best possible scenario that the two of you can create together.

A friend of mine who is a movie producer once commented, "There are only five major scripts in Hollywood. Every film is a different version of the same five stories that are continually being told in different ways." I thought, "Funny, that's how relationships are! Whenever a couple is enacting a drama, it always comes down to the same five scripts."

Here are the five scripts. Learn them, use them, and let them guide you away from missteps and misunderstandings and toward the man and life you want.

YOU ARE KEEPING THINGS FROM ME (a mystery thriller!): In this script, the man is convinced that there is something you are leaving out. It could be the details of the last conversation you had with your best friend. It could be the fun you had with coworkers at a recent lunch to which he was not invited. In this frequently rehearsed script, he accuses you of withholding the truth, while you either fall silent or present him with excessive details to assuage his anxiety. But if you compulsively tell him about the five stores you perused while shopping, but forget to tell him about the sixth (and he sees the receipt from that store), forget it! You are *done*, because you have now confirmed his belief and there is nothing you can do.

YOU ARE NEVER THERE FOR ME (a classic tearjerker): In this script, you are made to believe that you are rejecting or unavailable. When you spend time with friends, you hear, "You prefer others to me" or "I'm last on your list." In order to disconfirm your ill-fitting role, you might cancel plans, relinquish control, and rush to take care of him. You might even move in with him or get married in order to shut him up. But to your dismay, he continues to feel dismissed.

WITHOUT ME, YOU'D BE NOTHING (a farce): In this script, you become Eliza Doolittle in *My Fair Lady*. Although you are smart and accomplished, you are made to believe that you owe everything to him. When you throw a successful party, he compliments you for following his suggestions. And when you wear a trendy dress, he comments that your style has improved since the two of you began dating. If you listen carefully to this man, you might believe that your life would be a disaster without his help. Or that he is the only person who can meet your needs. Forget about shining in the role that this man has written for you. In his drama, he is always the lead.

GOLD DIGGER (a not-so-romantic comedy): In this script, you are made to feel that you are after his money, a commitment, or anything else that you can get your hands on. Phrases such as "Take, take, take" and "Everybody wants something from me" (directed toward others but secretly aimed at you) pepper this man's speech. And the belief that you are going to suck him dry is reflected in his belief that all you want is marriage, that you are going to divorce him and leave him high and dry (after he's transformed your life into something amazing), and that you only love him for what he can give. In this man's script, the woman is always greedy and never motivated by love.

MOMMY IN THE KITCHEN (a melodrama): The man who writes this script believes that you will always wait, no matter what he does. And that you will always be in love, regardless of how he treats you. Sure, he may dangle a carrot and offer a glimmer of hope whenever he fears that you might be slipping away. But in this playwright's mind, you are forever stand-ing in the kitchen with a spatula in one hand and a skillet in the other (or substitute: waiting by the phone while he shoots pool, hanging out at home while he goes to a strip club, slaving away at work while he plans a trip to Cabo with his buddies).

In this man's mind, it is *inconceivable* that you would be doing anything other than waiting for him! And it is difficult for him to imagine that you have a separate life. If you want to plan a night on the town with your friends just to get a reaction, don't. Because he'll either get crazy or he'll believe that you are still at home waiting for him—even if you're not.

The best way to get out of The Scriptwriter's box is to be yourself and go on with your life. When you act out a script, you erase the natural understandings that should be present in a relationship. Thus, even when you become angry, reexplain yourself, and present him with contradictory evidence, he will find it difficult to change his mind. Because the play has been scripted by him and acted out by you, he will never be open to new understandings about you.

(LITMUS TEST)

The Scriptwriter often thinks: *If I believe something, it must be true.*

For instance:
> *If I fear that you might suffocate me, you are suffocating me.*
> *If I feel that you do not care about my feelings, you are insensitive.*
> *If I fear that you are stupid, you are stupid.*

The Scriptwriter turns feelings into facts, and fears into realities. He imagines that he "knows" your true motivations, regardless of what you tell him. This man can be irritating and impossible because you're often stuck with *his* impressions of you.

[Gina's story]

Ray believed that Gina was shallow and frivolous, despite the fact that she had graduated from college and built her own business. In his mind, it didn't matter. She was still shallow and frivolous.

One day Ray spotted a sofa that he wanted for his home. Over several hours, he pressured Gina to "go in" with him. "How come you can never make a financial commitment?" "What else are you going to spend the money on? Clothing?" Even though Gina knew that she had been cast in the role of ditzy-girl-who-hoards-all-of-her-money-for-herself, she felt she couldn't argue. She whipped out her credit card and solidified her role.

Amazingly, Ray believed that Gina was financially irresponsible despite all the evidence to the contrary. For instance, he never said to himself, *I* fear *that Gina is shallow and frivolous, even though I know that this is not true.* Rather, he thought, *I know that Gina is careless, and she will never convince me otherwise.*

It was not until Gina worked up the courage to say no and be authentically herself that she was able to see that his scriptwriting was a serious problem.

If he continually makes up his own mind about you, and if he is closed to the suggestion that there has been a misunderstanding, it is a deal breaker. If he can acknowledge his misperceptions, and if he is open to new information about you, then it is a less serious problem and can be more easily worked on.

(WHO CHOOSES THIS TYPE OF MAN?)

Why do you choose men who are not attuned to you? I'll tell you: *Because you don't know any better.* And that is what this book is about. It is written to help you better understand his personality, identify bad patterns that you have established in your relationships with men, and bring to consciousness how these patterns got set in motion.

When in the past did you first experience the feelings that are engendered by the relationship you are now in? Do the men you have been choosing remind you of somebody?

Was it your parents, who decided who you were and never gave you the space to disagree, or become the person you were meant to be? Was it a traumatic event? Or a role you had to play in order to be loved? Was it caretakers who misread your cues and failed to understand what you were telling them? A mother who thought you were being defiant when you were merely expressing yourself? A father who thought you were out of control when you were just growing up or having a good time?

Keep in mind that these are the questions you should ask when the honeymoon is over, and you begin to recognize in him and in yourself the echoes of old stories and of past relationships that went awry. Let yourself feel that this time you want it to be different.

Reflect upon these questions when you no longer want to feel misunderstood because it gives you a fight to pick or a battle to wage. Or when you no longer want the role in which you have been cast to become your only identity. Or when you no longer desire a relationship arrangement that makes you feel angry and thus causes you to miss out on intimacy and closeness.

(WHEN IS IT A DEAL BREAKER?)

If you are with a Scriptwriter, how do you know if it is a deal breaker? If it is a deal breaker, everything will be full of hidden meanings and you will feel unable to dissuade him. For instance, when he says, "I like your new violet eye shadow," he really means, "I know you're hot for that waiter."

In his mind, a breast augmentation is not just a breast

augmentation. A breast augmentation is something you undergo because you secretly want to improve yourself so that you can find somebody new. Sex is never just sex. Sex is something you must do to reassure him. And a joke is never just a joke. A joke is something you may have told in order to humiliate him in front of his friends. Remember: A deal breaker is a standstill or negative arrangement. If the problem is workable, he will reflect upon it and use it as a tool for positive change. If it is not, he will be unable or unwilling to change it.

DEAL BREAKER SCENARIO: He never believes you. You try to rewrite the script. But at the end of the day, he never believes you, even when you try to rewrite the script.

WORK ON IT: When you correct him, he tries to understand what he's not getting. He is able to reflect upon the difference between his own fearful thoughts and the reality of who you are.

WALK AWAY: When you tell him that his characterization of you is wrong, he remembers the one time that you confirmed his perception. For instance, if he feels that you do not care about him (even though you are always sacrificing yourself for the relationship), he will remember the one night you stayed out too late and forgot to call him. He will throw historical events in your face, even though those events are not relevant to the current situation. Although you continually explain yourself, there is never a ray of sunshine or hope.

DEAL BREAKER SCENARIO: The relationship is full of constant reversals. He accuses you of being out of control, but he is out of control. He accuses you of flirting, but he continually flirts with women. After much arguing, you both spin out of control (and, hopefully, *he's* the one who spends the night on the couch).

WORK ON IT: You put a moratorium on inflammatory accusations, and he is able to agree. He observes that he is guilty of his own accusations. He owns the reversal, and begins to work on himself.

WALK AWAY: The more you try to defend yourself, the more evidence he gathers to confirm his point of view. He may even invoke God and the Scriptures to support his position! You become frightened to bring up painful subjects, for fear of sparking another argument.

DEAL BREAKER SCENARIO: You constantly fight because you are chronically misunderstood. For instance, when you ask him to back off, he feels that you are controlling him.

And when you explain that you are attempting to control your own life rather than his, he insists that you are wrong. Each misunderstanding leads to another.

WORK ON IT: He demonstrates a willingness to understand each misunderstanding from your point of view (even if he disagrees) and calls for professional help because he doesn't want to lose you.

WALK AWAY: His thinking never shifts, and his views are always right—no matter what you say. After you leave the relationship, you rarely fight with another partner again. In hindsight, you realize that the fighting was merely a reaction to constantly being misunderstood.

DEAL BREAKER SCENARIO: He is the only person in your life who feels that you are bad or that you harbor ill intentions. Although you are adored by family and friends, and everyone thinks that you have led an exemplary life, he never lets you out of the "bad" cage.

WORK ON IT: When you let him know that you feel framed, or that you are paying for a crime that you did not commit, he realizes that he is holding you responsible for the treatment that he's experienced at the hands of others. For instance, when you say, "For God's sake, I'm not your mother! She treated you that way, but I certainly don't!" he is able to say, "You're right, and I'm sorry that I've confused you with her."

WALK AWAY: When you point out the discrepancy between how he views you and how others view you, he insists that he knows the "real" you. He begins to view your friends and family with suspicion because they do not support his views. He refuses to attend a family dinner or say anything nice, just to prove his point that you are bad.

(IF YOU SUSPECT HE IS A SCRIPTWRITER)

The experience of being misunderstood can turn into a perpetual addiction, like that shoe that pinches your toes: You know it can't be fixed, yet you refuse to get rid of it because you like it. Sometimes a role becomes so familiar that it is difficult to give up. Especially if you know that your scriptwriter might leave and find a new actor to cast in his leading role. So at the very beginning of a relationship, you must be diligent. Understand his personality. Familiarize yourself with the patterns that both of you are repeating. Do not let one misunderstanding build upon another. And do not let his false perceptions fester.

From the very first encounter, pay attention to how he

makes you feel about yourself (this is the best diagnostic tool that you will ever have). Ask yourself, *Does he make me feel special? Unique? Insecure? Invisible? Doubtful? Uneasy?*

A man should never make you feel feelings you would not normally feel, unless it is the feeling of being special and desirable. And he should never, ever make you feel bad about yourself—especially if you have just met and he does not really know you. If he casts you in a role that feels uncomfortable—and if he, and only he, makes you feel this way—it is a deal breaker and you should run away as fast as possible.

The Man in Charge

CHAPTER 5

*The Man in Charge is intolerant toward people
and situations he cannot control.*

Do simple negotiations turn into power struggles? You tell him, "I'm going to a friend's house," and he responds, "You should have told me earlier." You know he's being controlling, but you give in and stay home in order to avoid a fight. You've lost your initiative, and you don't know how to regain it.

The Man in Charge has more rules than the IRS and becomes anxious when you do not conform to his plan. He feels mistrustful toward people and situations not under his direct influence or control. Thus, he may insist on being in the know about important aspects of your life. He may become worried if he cannot comment on your private conversations, check your schedule, or read your e-mails. He may even believe that without his help, you could not handle your own affairs or successfully negotiate your life. He is, of course, wrong.

(FIRST IMPRESSIONS)

At the beginning of your relationship you may observe that The Man in Charge is flexible and reliable in a few key areas. You admire this and begin to rely on his help. When he phones in advance to give you directions to the restaurant where you will be meeting or calls you afterward to make sure you got home safely, you find yourself saying, "Finally, a man who cares enough to be concerned about my life!"

As you make normal mistakes, however, you buttress his belief that you are not fully capable and that he should be in charge. Evidence of your mistakes (the harmless flirtation, the occasional bounced check, the freak car accident, or the over-the-top purchase) will eventually be thrown in your face whenever you express your autonomy or independence. Or he could begin to question your independent decisions.

Although you were initially relieved to know that he cared, you eventually begin to feel controlled, intruded upon, and smothered as he selectively directs certain aspects of your life. Your heart sinks when you begin to realize that independent actions are subjected to mistrust. For instance, you learn that if he is emotionally insecure, he may insist upon being present when you're with friends. And if he is concerned about money, he may ask you how much you spent on your last pair of shoes. If he is anxious about not being in the driver's seat, he may insist upon driving so that you will not get into an accident (unfortunately, his belief that you are a bad driver makes you swerve and weave, thus reinforcing his belief that you are not to be trusted behind the wheel).

This man's controlling stance is a reaction to profound anxiety. And in more severe cases, it is a method of using your weaknesses against you in order to assume a position of power and control. His actions are firmly rationalized, and he may sincerely believe that you cannot succeed without him.

When you get to know him, you discover that one or both of his parents dominated him. They never allowed him to assert himself, so he never learned to express himself in appropriate ways. Instead, he learned to control others before they could control him. Thus, he stays in charge because he is afraid of ever being made to feel helpless or powerless again.

You may discover that one or both of his parents were themselves out of control. Perhaps they were alcoholics. Or rage-oholics. Or spendaholics. And you realize that your partner came to feel that without his intervention, they would not be okay. And this is how he came to feel that he must be in charge of everybody and everything—including you.

[Chantal's story]

When Chantal met Owen, her life was in disarray. She had just graduated from college, was living in a small apartment, had not yet found a job, and was struggling to pay her bills. Like a hero, Owen swooped in and rescued her.

Within a year they moved in together. Chantal got a job as an executive assistant and Owen began working for the local fire department. On an unconscious level, Owen struggled with the fear that Chantal was irresponsible. This was never articulated overtly, but when Chantal pressed "snooze" on her alarm, Owen anxiously awakened her so that she would not be late. When Chantal went shopping, Owen asked for her receipts so that he could log them into a spreadsheet upon which he tracked all of their expenditures. And when Chantal decided to try a new salon, Owen quickly Googled the address so that she would not get lost. When Chantal asked him to back off, he reminded her that when they met, she had been irresponsible.

What's *wrong* with this picture? Underneath all that control, Owen believed that Chantal could not be trusted. And underneath his fear that Chantal could not be trusted was a deeper fear that the world was unreliable (because this was how he was made to feel as a child). And underneath his fear that the world was unreliable rested a deeper belief that it was all up to him to keep everything and everybody on track. This made Owen a great fireman, but an intrusive and controlling boyfriend.

(WARNING SIGNS)

This is what it is like to be in a relationship with The Man in Charge:

- He feels compelled to check up on you through texting and phone calls. If you don't respond, he becomes alarmed until he tracks you down.

- He continually offers suggestions and advice. He tells you how many drinks you can have. Or that your low-rider jeans are too low. (I mean, you didn't join the gym for nothin'!)

- He gets frustrated if you follow the serviceman's advice while purchasing your tires. He can't believe you didn't call him first, and he reminds you that he won't be there to pick up the pieces when rubber starts flying all over the road.

- Although he insists that you are a "good girl," there is that one person or activity that he just can't stand and considers a bad influence. Perhaps it is the yoga instructor who teaches you the power of connecting to "self." Or the free-spirited girlfriend who loves to take you out for margaritas on a Friday night.

• He has a philosophy or program to which he insists you must adhere. Perhaps it is an accounting program to track all your expenditures (but when he asks, "Where's the checkbook?" he really means, "You can't count past your fingers"). Or a diet and exercise routine to keep you from gaining weight. Or a Bible study that reminds you of your purpose.

• He inserts himself into important areas of your life. For instance, he checks out your blouse to make sure your breasts aren't exposed. Or he talks over you while you are on the phone with friends. Or he packs your lunch so that you won't "spend money you don't have" or go out and have fun with coworkers (he's a buzzkill).

The Man in Charge creates environments in which you must be sneaky in order to have your own private self, friendships, and plans. But watch out! Because if he discovers that you have kept something from him, his misperception that you are untrustworthy will be reinforced and he will have a new weapon to wield against you.

(HOW TO KNOW IF HE'S A MAN IN CHARGE)

Are you afraid to accept a personal invitation or make a decision without first checking with him? On some level you know that his control is not right—but you feel too intimidated to talk to him about it? Your friends are able to plan a last-minute get-together, but you are afraid to go with them because he might get mad? These are the telltale signs that he is a Man in Charge.

The Man in Charge believes he has superior mastery of most situations. Why? Perhaps he was raised by parents who were chaotic, absent, or interfering and he came to fear that they were not reliable. Or that they would not get things right. Thus, he now prefers plans and activities that come from him. If you accept a dinner invitation without first checking with him, he might become angry. And if you bring home a new dress without having first asked his opinion, he may criticize it. Even if you surprise him by planning a vacation or choosing a new restaurant, he might react negatively. His need to feel that everything emanates from him may inhibit going to new places, making unexpected friends, and enjoying exciting adventures. He experiences plans that do not first meet with his approval as an attempt to take over.

[Kate's story]

When Kate met Justin, she knew on some level that he was rigid and controlling. But he was a well-respected engineer, and she understood that his obsessive traits were helpful in his profession.

Fast-forward one year. Although the beginning of their relationship had been steamy and torrid, they had stopped having sex and Justin rarely complimented Kate. Hoping to rekindle the passion, Kate bought a pair of sexy underwear, thigh-high stockings, and a flirty cocktail dress. After dinner one night, she threw off the dress and pranced around the bedroom in her thigh-highs. Justin was aghast! What had happened to the Kate he knew? Had someone gotten a hold of her and made her feel sexy? And what about that cocktail dress? Had she gotten some extra money and gone shopping when he wasn't looking? And what about her timing? How could she be so insensitive as to surprise him, when sex was the furthest thing from his mind?

Understandably, Kate did not yet fully comprehend the tortured fantasies that she had unleashed. So the next day, Kate called her friends and cried because she felt unattractive and humiliated.

In therapy Kate asked, "Is it him or is it me?" I educated Kate about the fact that Justin needed to be the originator of everything and therefore could never open himself to new experiences. So Kate posed the questions we're all faced with in frustrating situations: "What shall I do about it? Should I work on it or walk away? How can I know if this is a deal breaker?"

I answered, "Explain to Justin that he refuses to accept anything other than his own plans and that the relationship will never flourish if he cannot embrace your spontaneous, exciting self! If he can *observe his rigidity and understand how it makes you feel*, pick one agreed-upon area in which he has been closed-minded. Perhaps it is his unwillingness to go to your favorite restaurant. Or to socialize with your best friend, whom he finds annoying. Once you have agreed upon one specific area, ask him to incorporate that person or activity into the relationship. If he cares enough to accommodate, the relationship can succeed. But if he is unwilling to relinquish his tight grip, how could this relationship possibly move forward without tremendous cost to your happiness? And how could you spend your life with someone who cares more about making his point than being thoughtful toward you?"

(MORE WARNING SIGNS)

• If you do not follow his instructions (for instance, use the credit card of his choice or follow a route he has mapped), he will feel agitated and upset, yet be unable to observe that he is interfering.

• Because he is so confident about his "managerial skills," he will remind you as soon as you fail to fulfill a task to his satisfaction. For instance, he may ask you to make dinner reservations. But then he will jump in and remind you before you have had time to pick up the phone. And when you point out that he is being controlling, he will shout, "What's wrong? Why are you always questioning me instead of doing what I ask?" And when you comment that he is checking up on you instead of trusting you to be a responsible adult, he will say, "But you told me it would be done by now! Why do I continually have to remind you?" Then he will support his argument by reminding you of the last time you failed to follow his instructions (even if that was two years ago).

• He will continually interrupt you, especially when you are enjoying yourself. In his mind, separateness—independence—is a threat because it allows you to have your own experience and potentially disagree with him. This does not make him happy!

• This man can be paranoid when it comes to your sexuality. Although it is your femininity and sensuality that attracted him in the first place, he feels anxious and out of control whenever you express your sexuality or freely display your assets. He may button up your blouse, shut down your flirtations (even if you're flirting with him in the privacy of your own home), criticize your makeup, and cut you off from friends who think you're sexy.

• Mr. Follow-My-Rules is incredibly repetitive. Once he sets his sights on an important issue (like your unwillingness to stop chatting on the cell phone while driving), he will continually remind you that you could get into an accident. And when you ask him to stop reminding you, he will accuse you of not listening or valuing his advice. If you inform him that you do not want to be nagged, he will tell you that he will not be there if you have an accident and find yourself in the ER (because it will be your fault for not listening).

(LITMUS TEST)

A good way to determine if he's The Man in Charge is to ask him to embrace an activity that you have been planning and he has been rejecting. Don't do a lot of preplanning or prefinessing. Just make a spontaneous plan, and see if he can be flexible and good-natured about it.

Because here's the paradox: The Man in Charge is terrified of being told what to do. Like the Cowardly Lion in *The Wizard of Oz*, he is frightened by new experiences and unfamiliar situations and lacks the courage to face his fears. In fact, one of the reasons he controls you is that he is afraid of being controlled and of being exposed to situations that he can't handle. Perhaps his parents subjected him to unwanted or overwhelming situations during childhood, such as alcoholism, traumatic events, constant verbal directions, strict rules, and so on. And whenever you ask him to accommodate you, he once again feels intruded upon. Or that he has lost his will.

The Man in Charge believes that if he is in charge of you, you will never be in charge of him. And that if everything stems from him, he will never be forced to bend to your will. Although he appears intimidating and authoritative, he is unable to graciously concede without feeling small, manipulated, and helpless. The Man in Charge is so afraid of being dominated he cannot be spontaneous or responsive. Tell this man what to do, and he feels emasculated or angry.

[Perry's story]

Perry is a midlevel manager at a large department store. He has a super-reasonable girlfriend and a large circle of friends. Perry came to therapy because his girlfriend told him that if he didn't stop controlling her, she was going to leave. I soon discovered that beneath his authoritative exterior, Perry was terrified of being told what to do. In fact, Perry was so afraid of being controlled that he was in danger of losing his job! If his boss told him to wear a tie, Perry would reluctantly comply but then rebel by loosening it to the point that he looked sloppy. And when his girlfriend asked him to set the table for a dinner party, Perry would grudgingly agree but place the forks at odd angles and refuse to set the table until the very last minute. In therapy it became apparent that the controller was terrified of being controlled.

(EVEN MORE WARNING SIGNS)

• Mr. Withholding adopts a rigid stance in order to avoid an experience of being coerced. For instance, he may refuse to spend extra money or pay you a compliment (*especially* if you want him to).

• He ruins an important night (dinner with your boss) by picking a petty argument (he is mad at you because you were five minutes late). Or he diminishes a special gift (you cook him dinner) by criticizing it ("The meat loaf was a little dry"). He does this because he feels that you are subjecting him to a distressing situation, as has happened so many times before in his life. Or because he feels that you can't get anything right.

• He presents you with a series of questions whenever he is losing ground on a deeply cherished issue. For instance, if he is afraid that you have spent too much money on an outfit, he will ask, "Where did you buy that?" "Was it last Saturday that you went shopping?" "Did you go to other stores as well?" "Did you check to see if it was on sale?" "Under what category of the budget should I categorize this?" His questioning discourages you from exercising your own judgment.

• He is comforted by his refusal to give in! Flexibility is not his strong suit.

• Although you continually argue about the same subject, his answers never vary. For instance, if you want to go to couples counseling, he will say, "Why should I pay someone to tell me what I already know?" This rationale is continually presented without variation or change, no matter how you present your argument. There is always a power struggle and rarely a dialogue. Although small advances are made, the larger issue remains.

• When you ask him to stop interfering, he accuses *you* of controlling *him*. For instance, he tells you to skip dessert because you have been complaining about your weight. When you tell him that you do not need to be reminded, he accuses you of controlling him by limiting what he can say. He does not link your reactions with how he has treated you.

[Victoria's story]

Every New Year's, Victoria cooks a gourmet dinner for her girlfriends. Each friend brings a bottle of wine, an appetizer, or a dessert. The party has become a yearly ritual, and is the one time that all of her friends gather. They gossip, laugh, and have fun.

Over time the party has become a problem for Victoria's controlling fiancé, who doesn't eat dessert, doesn't drink alcohol, and resents the money that she spends entertaining (life o' the party he ain't). He knows he can't forbid her to have the party. Instead, he waits until the party is in full swing and righteously walks through the living room in smelly gym clothes, holding an energy drink and gobbling a plate of tofu and salmon.

When Victoria finally came to therapy, she said, "I wish he would support the things that make me happy. Am I asking for too much?" I responded, "How can the relationship work if he can never be generous? Or if he only supports the things that do not cost him anything? If he is willing to contribute, then the relationship has possibility. But if he feels that he should never be put out, I do not hold out much hope."

(WHO CHOOSES THIS TYPE OF MAN?)

Perhaps you are with The Man in Charge because you, too, were raised by overbearing or domineering parents who did not teach you to stand up for yourself. You are so familiar with the experience of being intruded upon, given advice, and resisted that you ignore the fact that you have lost control of your life! And it is only when you are in the presence of loving friends or wise mentors that you realize you have lost your voice. But when you try to disentangle yourself from the relationship, he draws you in, and the helpful voices are quickly dismissed and forgotten.

When you fall in love with a controller, you live life with the volume turned down on your inner voice. You are easily brainwashed and are made to believe that your wish for independence is a betrayal of the relationship arrangement to which you originally agreed.

When you choose a Man in Charge, you are continually made to pay for the petty crime of having a personality. You come to imagine that if you were more accommodating, he would be more giving. And if you hadn't slipped up and betrayed him, he would give you more freedom. What you don't realize is that you are serving an endless jail sentence.

It is not until you are able to pose the question, "What am I giving up by being in this relationship?" that you are able to emancipate yourself and reach for the freedom that you deserve.

(WHEN IS IT A DEAL BREAKER?)

When The Man in Charge first meets you, he is drawn to your sparkly and unique personality. He accommodates you because you are exciting and you make his life better. But over time, the traits that he initially found appealing (your witty remarks, your ability to talk comfortably with strangers) will begin to feel threatening. And he will attempt to control and squash your independent, fabulous self.

DEAL BREAKER SCENARIO: There is one bridge he will not cross, because he refuses to give in. Perhaps he won't move in together or participate in an important area of your life. Perhaps he won't spend the night in your bed. Or trust you to manage your own schedule. But unless he crosses this bridge, the relationship is doomed.

WORK ON IT: Although the bridge might be scary, he wants to reach the other side. He realizes that unless he takes that first step, he can never get closer to you. The relationship is prized above all, even above his personal agenda.

WALK AWAY: No matter how many times you ask him to cross the bridge, he presents the same argument and the answer never changes. Although you long for flexibility and collaboration, he remains resolute and continues to resist you.

DEAL BREAKER SCENARIO: He worms his way into every part of your life, even when he is not invited. For instance, he asks for the password to your e-mail account. Or he tries to influence your friendships. Every part of your life is fair game.

WORK ON IT: When you draw the line (for instance, when you tell him that you want to choose your own friends), he backs off. Although he wants to be in the know about every-thing, he makes strides toward understanding that you have a private self and can be trusted.

WALK AWAY: He does not respect the concept of privacy. When you refuse him access to your e-mail, voice mail, or private conversations, he becomes worried that you are cheating or talking about him. He strong-arms you through intimidation or gains access to your e-mail by offering to help you with your Internet service. Whenever you hesitate, he responds, "What are you hiding?"

DEAL BREAKER SCENARIO: He fears that you have bad judgment or believes that you cannot be trusted to make your own decisions. Because of this, he continually offers unsolicited and unwanted advice.

WORK ON IT: When you explain that you are an adult capable of making your own decisions, he hears you. When you ask him to respect your independence, he realizes that his anxieties have been distorting his assessment of you.

WALK AWAY: No matter how many times you let him know that you do not want to be patronized, he reinforces the message *I am the boss of you.*

(IF YOU SUSPECT HE IS A MAN IN CHARGE)

Ultimately, the only means of determining if you should work on it or walk away is to have a conversation. Tell him that he has been controlling, and that the relationship will not survive if he does not occasionally give in. If he cares, he will respond. He may respond in small ways at first. He may reply by allowing you to make a decision in one key area of your life. Or by accepting an idea he has been rejecting. Or by admitting that you are an adult capable of making your own decisions. The change may not be immediate or dramatic—but he should demonstrate the willingness to try.

Once again, let me spell it out.

DEAL BREAKER SCENARIO: He runs your relationship like a small country (and one with a boring flag at that). He is the dictator and you are his subject. You're mad as hell, and you're not going to take it anymore.

WORK ON IT: You tell him that he is no longer solely in charge. To your surprise, he concedes that he has been overbearing and modifies his behavior in order to save the relationship. He also learns to tolerate a difference of opinion and the mutual exchange of ideas. Although he struggles with issues of control, he realizes that a good relationship is a dialogue and not a dictatorship, that liberty is a universal right, and that freedom of speech is more than a political ideal.

WALK AWAY: When you say, "Back off, Fidel, I don't need to be told what to do," he responds, "Don't tell *me* not to tell you what to do. *You're* the one who is controlling!"

When he denies that he is a dictator, and loves telling you what to do, it is time to go to into exile or to seek political asylum. Or "emigrate" to that hot guy who flirts with you at the gym.

The Man Without Fault

The Man Without Fault believes he is more important than everyone else. He cannot self-reflect and rarely takes responsibility for his actions and feelings.

Does your relationship revolve around him? Does he revel in his wonderfulness while you bask in his glow? Or wither in his shadow?

Perhaps you look up to him and feel that he has something special that nobody else has. But as time passes, you question whether his view is the only view. Or whether his valuable qualities are as unique as you thought. Perhaps you want to feel special, but the relationship has room for only one ego.

The Man Without Fault views himself as unique and above reproach. He feels that he is remarkable and that others should automatically admire him. He overvalues his achievements, dismisses his shortcomings, and minimizes the negative impact that his behavior has on others.

Regardless of his accomplishments or his status in life, The Man Without Fault feels that he *is* the best, that he *knows* the best, and that he *comes from* the best.

(FIRST IMPRESSIONS)

When you first meet The Man Without Fault, you are made to feel that his life is more valuable than those around him. You might even believe that his house is better built, his religious dedication is deeper, his insurance business is more successful, his managerial skills are more effective, his salesmanship is slicker, his sportsmanship is unparalleled, or that he is quite simply more impressive than others. And by association, you believe that you are special too. Your belief in your own uniqueness is reinforced by his initial willingness to favor you and treat you like a queen.

At the beginning, you notice that he is verbal and willing to discuss issues. But over time, you also notice that he does not look inward, does not see himself as the agent of any of the problems in his life, and cannot see the impact he has on others. This frustrates you because he never feels that he has done anything wrong. Even when he is hurtful, he is comfortable with how he conducts his life and how he treats others. He lives in an unrealistic world that is governed by the sentiment that he is above reproach.

For example, he may say mean things, but then deny that he was hurtful. He may talk about himself exclusively, but then be clueless about the fact that he is self-absorbed. He may drink excessively or stay out all night without calling, but feel that you should deal with it. He may avoid commitment but then be unable to understand that he has wasted your time.

At the beginning of a relationship with The Man Without Fault, he will adore you, idealize you, win and woo you, compliment you—because you are the prize! But over time, he will prop himself up through the never-ending process of diminishing your contributions and questioning your worth. And the once beautiful "you" will be replaced by a drab little "nothing" who feels confused about how she lost her sense of self.

When you begin to wonder how he came to be this way, you might discover that his caretakers were devaluing and critical. As a reaction to how small they made him feel, he defensively took flight into imagining that he was flawless and above reproach. As an adult, he might have even adopted a role (perhaps of leader, guide, or guru). His role helps him establish a sense of himself as superior and allows him to disguise his disavowed feelings of being a loser.

The Man Without Fault clings to beauty and perfection

as a way of clinging to the illusion that *he* is beautiful and perfect. As he does so, however, he also turns you into the small, worthless person he was once made to feel like as a child. When it comes to what you have to offer, nothing is ever good enough.

(WARNING SIGNS)

Over time The Man Without Fault may begin to treat you shabbily. And you may begin to feel that you can't bring anything up without feeling like a complainer. Because The Man Without Fault isn't self-examining or introspective, he cannot respond appropriately to your needs or your dissatisfactions (that's the "without fault" part). If you ask him for more time, he may feel that he has given enough. And if you try to discuss relationship problems, he may feel that there is nothing wrong or accuse you of taking advantage of him.

The Man Without Fault will feel most interested in you when you are serving a purpose in his life—for instance, when you are running his errands or putting him through college. If you try to confront him about this, however, he may deflect the conversation in order to conceal the problem or deny his own shortcomings.

[Lisa's story]

Lisa and John came to therapy after three months of dating (keep in mind—if you have to seek counseling in the first few months, it could be a deal breaker). Though John had initially been enamored of Lisa, he was becoming unenthusiastic about anything other than his own friends and interests.

Lisa: "We used to go to dinner parties. But now it's almost impossible to get a commitment out of John. My best friends asked us to dinner last Friday. But John never got back to me, so I had to turn them down."

John: "I didn't know that you wanted to get together with them. You should have told me."

Lisa: "I *did* tell you. But you got so irritated that I dropped the subject."

John: "Are you saying I avoided you? How was I supposed to know that you were obsessing about going out with your friends?"

Lisa: "But you drop the subject whenever I bring it up. What am I supposed to do about that?"

John: "I told you that if you tell me about invitations on Monday, then I will let you know by Wednesday if I really want to go."

Lisa: "That's what I did the week before when we were invited to that cocktail party."

John: "But the people who were throwing that party are so shallow and pretentious."

As I listened to Lisa and John, I noticed that he went to great lengths to deflect her concerns. And when he could do it no longer, he resorted to devaluing her and her friends.

At the beginning of their relationship, John had wined and dined Lisa. But now that he had her, she was no longer a valuable commodity. And the more she tried to get him to talk about it, the more callous and indifferent he became.

Because The Man Without Fault cannot allow himself to be cast in a negative light, he may not admit to any hurt he has caused. If you say, "Your comment hurt my feelings," he may say, "I didn't say anything wrong!" or "You don't appreciate anything I do!" He may even begin to blame his problem on others or on you.

The Man Without Fault finds it difficult to change because change requires personal reflection.

This is how conversations go with a man who cannot self-reflect:

SHE SAYS: It made me feel bad when you got so angry in front of our friends. I know I made a mistake, but you could have waited to point it out. Now I feel embarrassed about the scene we made.

HE SAYS: You are always worrying about what others think! What did you expect, when you made such a terrible mistake? I'm sick and tired of hearing you complain, especially when you are the one who messed up in the first place.

WHAT YOU NEED HIM TO SAY: I'm sorry I embarrassed you in front of our friends. I was upset about your mistake, but I should have controlled myself and waited until we were alone.

SHE SAYS: I feel like you make plans but don't include me. I know your friends are important, but I would love to be invited along at least some of the time. The other men invite their girlfriends, but I am never asked.

HE SAYS: You're so needy. I would ask, but I never know ahead of time when we are going to get together. Besides, the places we go aren't really the right environment for a woman. It's mostly a guy situation.

WHAT YOU NEED HIM TO SAY: I'm sorry I've been excluding you. I guess I get carried away and plan things at the last minute. But I can see that it is not the right thing to do. I'll try harder next time.

SHE SAYS: I would love it if you helped me around the house. I work all day, and then I come home and work some more. I don't mind doing my part, but sometimes I feel like I'm a single mother and you are my *child*!

HE SAYS: You're always thinking about yourself. I work too, you know. Besides, I make more money than you do. You could try being a little more considerate.

WHAT YOU NEED HIM TO SAY: Sorry, honey. I've let things slide. Tell me what I can do to make life easier for you.

SHE SAYS: I'd like to know where this relationship is headed. I'm thirty years old, and I need to think about my future. Do you think we'll ever get married and start a family?

HE SAYS: I was just beginning to relax and be in the moment, and you ruined it! You bring things up at the worst possible time. All you do is pressure, pressure, pressure! Do you think I would be with you if I didn't think we could be together?

WHAT YOU NEED HIM TO SAY: Let's talk about it.

SHE SAYS: You always stomp around the house as if you are angry. I feel like I'm on pins and needles, and that I have to be careful so you won't react. Sometimes I wonder if I've done something wrong. It's very stressful.

HE SAYS: What do you want me to do? Put on a happy face and pretend that nothing is wrong?

WHAT YOU NEED HIM TO SAY: I didn't realize that I was having such a big impact on you. I've been feeling upset because (fill in the blank). Next time, I'll tell you what's wrong instead of taking it out on you.

The inability to self-reflect underscores almost every personality style that leads to a deal breaker. And in almost every chapter, you will hear the echoes of the themes that I just described. The capacity to self-reflect is important because *healthy relationships are flexible relationships*. And introspection paves the way for flexibility and change. Throughout the course of a relationship, you will have plenty of opportunity to notice if your partner looks inward and thinks about his contribution to problems, or if he looks outward and casts all the blame upon you. If he thinks about the issues that make you unhappy, then annoying problems won't turn into deal breakers! If he is the type of man who couldn't see himself in a three-way mirror with department store lighting, however, then you will have two deal breakers: 1) the original problem that is bothering you, and 2) his inability to think about it!

(HOW TO KNOW IF HE'S A MAN WITHOUT FAULT)

Does everything revolve around him? Although you both have friends, jobs, and a life—his friends, job, and life are better? And when you ask him for respect, you leave the conversation feeling worse than you did before?

The primary feature of The Man Without Fault's personality is an inflated sense of self-importance and a devaluing attitude toward others. In other words, this man feels that he is precious! His philosophical outlook is better, his possessions are "nothing but the best," his ideas are loftier, his agenda is more important, his brand of religion is superior, and his mission is central to the welfare of all mankind (you may think I am kidding, but think about the preacher who feels that without his message, souls will perish . . . or the car mechanic who feels that without his tune-up, nobody will be safe on the road).

For example, I once met a physician who wanted to refer patients to my practice. During the initial meeting, he mentioned that his house had recently gained two hundred thousand dollars in value, that he was a Juilliard-trained pianist, that his patients were clamoring for his time, and that he had a new psychological theory that he—and only he—had thought up. Do you see where I am going with this?

Men with superiority complexes come in all shapes and

sizes. He may be an attorney who routinely crushes his opponents and then goes home and lawyers his wife and children in order to get his way. Or the starving artist whose work is superior but not yet recognized. Or the unrecognized better boss who has not yet been given the power that he deserves. The Man Without Fault is determined to be recognized as the brilliant success that he imagines himself to be.

[Madison's story]

Madison and Nick began dating while they were in law school. After graduation Madison took a job in a law firm while Nick began his own private law practice. In couples therapy, I was struck by Nick's arrogant attitude toward Madison.

Madison: "It is stressful for me, because Nick expects me to be available whenever he calls. He does not understand that I am in a corporate environment and that other people might be overhearing our conversations."

Nick: "Madison is a conformist who gives in to everybody. She bought into corporate America, while I was brave enough to strike out on my own. And she's everybody's work slave, while I am in charge of my own schedule. It disgusts me that she acts like her colleagues and clients are more important than I am."

Throughout the session, I was struck by the fact that

Nick felt his career and scheduling choices were superior to Madison's, that he was more in charge of his life, and that Madison was a less evolved person who should drop everything and everyone whenever he wanted.

I should let you know that the primary reason that Nick and Madison came to therapy was that his law practice was failing. As is the case with "faultless" men, Nick's perception that he was special and unique was insistent even when he was floundering. At the same time, Nick was critical of Madison for failing to match up to his idea of success.

This is what it is like to live with a man who has a superiority complex:

HIM: He asks you to devote a great deal of time and energy to a project that is important to him. He feels that you should equally share his interest in advancing his education, decorating his house, attending his church, watching his sports games, pimping his ride, spending time at his gym, entertaining his family and friends, cooking his favorite meals . . .

YOU: You feel that you are living his dream, not yours. You feel exhausted and used.

HIM: He makes you feel that you can never completely earn his love or find favor in his eyes.

YOU: You keep waiting for that golden egg of approval, but it never comes. You feel depleted when you finally realize that true reward or gratitude is never coming. Although the promise of a fuller relationship is continually held out, nothing moves forward and an acceptable commitment is never offered.

HIM: He feels that he is the only one capable of accomplishing greatness. His feelings of superiority may be hidden under a thin veil of modesty. But underneath, he believes that he is greater, bigger, better, smarter, and more talented.

YOU: You begin to lose a sense of your glamorous self.

HIM: He feels himself to be part of an elite group of people. His buddies, family, church, or culture are to him a special group of which he is a member.

YOU: At first you feel special too. But over time you feel picked apart in many little ways. You redouble your efforts in order to regain favor. You clean the house, try to be more thoughtful, and bring home small gifts. You keep hoping for the acknowledgment that you once had. You eventually realize that you are now diminished, although you were once prized.

(LITMUS TEST)

You know that he is a Man Without Fault. And you want to talk to him about the unequal distribution of power and worth in your relationship. But you fear that he will deflate at the smallest hint of disagreement or disapproval and then turn on you.

Does this sound like your man? He suffers from an unconscious sense of inadequacy, although he acts like he's bigger than God? And because of his fragile sense of self, he often gets his feelings hurt? And when you do something harmless, such as compliment a male friend, ask for time apart, express an opinion or need, or assert a difference of opinion, he feels wounded and insulted?

When a faultless man gets his feelings hurt, he often feels attacked. And when he feels attacked, he invariably attacks back—and *cruelly*—to shut you down.

This is because The Man Without Fault was raised by caretakers who only admired the parts of him that were important to them. They did not adequately supply him with admiring phrases and good feelings that he could later fall back upon when feeling criticized. Thus, even minor criticism is enough to take the wind out of his sails.

In severe cases, The Man Without Fault may become so reactive that he appears moralistic. For instance, if you comment that he has been insensitive, he may respond, "How can you complain, when I make more money than you?"

Beneath his thin facade of firmly rationalized outrage, however, is a small man who suffers from a lack of good feelings about himself.

[Sophia's story]

Sophia came to therapy to explore her "sexual problems." In the first session, she disclosed that her husband, Edward, was unhappy because she would not have sex as often as he wanted.

Upon exploration, I discovered that Sophia was an executive who worked full time and spent her extra time managing the household, cooking meals, and mothering their three young children. Her hands were full and her husband rarely helped.

Edward had once been a successful small-business owner. But his business had recently declined and he was tortured by the belief that other, less talented colleagues were succeeding at careers that rightfully should be his. Although Edward had once been the primary breadwinner, their roles were now reversed.

As Sophia spoke, I began to wonder if Edward had suffered a fatal blow to his self-esteem following his business failure. I also wondered if he got his feelings hurt whenever she refused to have sex. I suspected that Edward had little insight into how tired and overwhelmed Sophia felt at the end of the day. As is typical with faultless men, Edward saw himself and nobody else.

When I asked Sophia what she felt was upsetting her husband, she said, "Since his business fell apart, he has wanted to have sex every day. If I do not give in, he tells me that I do not love him and that he cannot take it anymore."

Because Edward was vulnerable to anything that poked a hole in his precarious self-esteem, he took Sophia's fatigue as a sign that he was not enough. He felt wounded and insulted, and went on the attack by accusing her of being frigid and emotionally unavailable.

Because faultless men are so vulnerable to getting their feelings hurt, there is often a negative cascading effect when they feel diminished or experience a temporary setback in their lives. It can be difficult to ask The Man Without Fault to meet your needs or do a special favor. Because he takes everything personally, he may hear your request as an inference that he has been inadequate. He might feel deflated and then set out to systematically deflate and dismantle you for exposing him to negative feelings about himself. The wish to seek revenge is the cornerstone of this man's personality.

For instance, you might say, "I would love to experiment sexually." But he may hear "You are not sexually exciting," and then get even by saying, "If you got a breast augmentation, perhaps I would feel more turned on and be more willing to experiment sexually."

Or you might say, "Honey, could we spend more time

talking?" and he could hear "You are not good enough" and then respond, "I can never win, no matter what I do! I can never win!"

The Man Without Fault will adore you as long as you are always a mirror for his wonderfulness. But as soon as he feels that the mirror has cracked, exposing him to his unconscious feelings of inadequacy, he will become ruthless in his unending quest to recover the power and adoration that he feels he once had.

Afraid that his inability to handle the truth is a deal breaker? Continue to tell him what you need! What is the worst thing that could happen? That he would react and his selfishness would be exposed? Or that you might need to take a cold, hard look at your need to suppress your personality in order to make him happy?

A workable relationship should consist of two people, with two separate yet occasionally intertwining agendas, and two sets of met needs.

(WHO CHOOSES THIS TYPE OF MAN?)

Ironically, it is your own need to be viewed as special and admirable that drives you to fall in love with this man. But as the relationship progresses and you begin to ask for more commitment, closeness, intimacy, or understanding, he begins to distort your good intentions and feel that you are insulting him. In his mind, the bloom is off the bud. During this phase you begin to feel confused. How could the man who once adored you now accuse you of thinking only of yourself? And how could you have gone from prize to peasant? You begin to feel hopeless and perhaps even begin to give up on yourself (you gain weight, stop taking care of yourself, give up your hopes and dreams, fail to reach out to friends). You feel reluctant to leave and reestablish your life for fear that he is right and that you would be nothing without him.

Over time you begin to feel that when he's good, you're good. When he's happy, you're happy. When he gives you crumbs of attention, you have been given a feast. And when he shines on you, you bask in the glow. But when he takes his affection away, you long for the sun to return. (Cut the cord—this guy is bad news and not worth all the crunches you're going to have to do once you wise up and begin taking off all that weight he made you gain.)

Sadly, it is your own addiction to approval that keeps you hooked in the relationship.

(WHEN IS IT A DEAL BREAKER?)

If it is a deal breaker, he will turn on a dime whenever he feels diminished or ignored. You will find it difficult to speak freely around him, because he will become reactive and attribute negative meanings to the most innocent of comments. You will begin to feel that you can never disagree or question (and certainly, you can *never* walk out of the room during a discussion), because he will feel upset.

If you feel that you are constantly walking on eggshells, you might want to reflect upon a few issues. Why are *your* concerns trivialized? Why are you afraid to bring them up? Why won't he allow you to talk about the lack of progress and reward in the relationship? Or about the circular arguments that go nowhere? Or about the overemphasis on his career and his life?

Although The Man Without Fault may feel picked on and persecuted, he will construct deal-breaking arrangements that deprive you and benefit only him. Here are some examples of deal breakers, when you should attempt to work on them, and when you should walk away:

DEAL BREAKER SCENARIO: He relishes the admiration of new acquaintances and strangers, while discounting your love and devotion.

WORK ON IT: He overvalues others because he is a legend in his own mind and both of you are getting rich off his career. Seriously—the only way to address this deal-breaking problem is to confront him about his adoration addiction. If the problem is workable, he will own it, understand it, and begin to change his behavior.

WALK AWAY: He gravitates toward strangers because he can spin new stories and be the big cheese. Meanwhile, he ignores you because you see through him. Despite your protestation about the inordinate time and energy that he devotes to others, he is not dissuaded. With dismay, you realize that his self-esteem rises and falls upon the smiles and frowns of strangers.

DEAL BREAKER SCENARIO: Whenever you express your needs, he feels offended and goes on the attack.

WORK ON IT: He is able to identify the fact that he feels offended because you have tapped into one of his core anxieties. Even when you lapse into asserting your needs in a militant or combative manner (because you have come to believe that he does not care), he tries to listen and respond.

WALK AWAY: He cannot listen without feeling criticized, so he launches a counteroffensive. The relationship never moves forward and nothing is ever resolved.

DEAL BREAKER SCENARIO: The life the two of you have created is more rewarding for him than it is for you.

WORK ON IT: Even if he has more friends or an exciting career, he is proud of your accomplishments and recognizes your contribution. He is also willing to change direction on a cherished goal or project so that it will be more fulfilling for both of you. When you wake up and realize that your life is not personally rewarding, he creates an atmosphere in which you can pursue your own dreams.

WALK AWAY: No matter how hard you work to help him plan his parties, decorate his house, dote on his mother, feather his nest, et cetera, there is no personal reward or furthering of the relationship. His future looks bright, while your future with him looks dim. No matter what you do, it's all about him and never about you.

DEAL BREAKER SCENARIO: You accompany him to a dinner party and realize that he is not as wonderful as you thought (especially when you compare him to the people he has been viciously devaluing). Or you realize that his wonderful intellect is not valued by his peers (though he told you it would be). Perhaps you take him home to meet your mother and she detects a deal-breaking flaw that was not apparent to you (she discovers it before you have finished the first course—and is quick to let you in on her discovery).

WORK ON IT: You realize that your own need for perfection has driven you to put him on a pedestal. Or that your wish to feel special and admirable has prompted you to idealize him so that you can bask in his wonderfulness and feel wonderful too. As you try to view him more realistically, however, you discover that his flaws are acceptable and that he is comfortable with himself. His previously undetected faults do not seem so bad after all.

WALK AWAY: His ego is so big that it has its own zip code. Because he exaggerates his value, when you refuse to flatter him he becomes unbearable to live with. He has a difficult time believing that automatic praise and admiration would not be forthcoming.

(IF YOU SUSPECT HE IS A MAN WITHOUT FAULT)

Regardless of the problem, it is a man's ability and willingness to seek solutions (such as changing his behavior or going to counseling) that determines whether you should work on it or walk away. And it is only after a full assessment of the negative impact upon your life that you can determine whether the problem is a minor quarrel or an ongoing crisis. If you go through your day thinking about relationship problems, worrying about your last fight, unable to focus or concentrate, upset about the cost to your future, doubtful about your outside relationships, and unsure about the direction the relationship is headed, then you need to confront the reality that you must work through your relationship impasse or it's time to get out the coffin!

Do you feel that without him you would be nothing? Or that if you left him your opportunities would diminish? Or that you would shrivel up and grow old in a hovel with a million cats and no one to love? Or be forced to learn how to knit and end up joining one of those dreadful "stitch and bitch" groups of sad, angry women? Wake up, silly! If the relationship is a deal breaker, then this is how he wants you to feel! He needs you to believe that you will only thrive in his garden. But if you are shriveling because he is hogging all the nutrients and blocking the sun, then perhaps you should uproot yourself and find a garden of your own. After all, the true sign that it is time to walk away is when you begin to put down new roots and your life finally begins to blossom.

The Invisible Man
CHAPTER 7

The Invisible Man is emotionally constricted and frequently
shuts down in the context of intimate relationships.

Do you fear that you are in love with an illusion? You long
for closeness, but he's never there? Or you work so hard to
create a sense of intimacy that you feel like you are doing all
the heavy lifting in the relationship? If so, it's likely you're
with The Invisible Man.

The Invisible Man's personality is emotionally constricted. Loving makes him feel vulnerable and exposed, and
he frequently shuts down in the context of intimate relationships. He prefers impersonal tasks and focuses primarily on
interests and activities that do not require social involvement.
The most frustrating feature of this man is his unwillingness
to feel. He may go to great lengths to avoid anger, excitement, or even the feeling of being in love. He may have few

friends and might avoid intimacy (although he might have sex if you want him to—what a trooper!). He prefers spending time by himself rather than with others. And he relishes the social isolation that most people fear.

The Invisible Man may exercise excessively, spend long hours on the computer or reading, or overly involve himself in business or sports activities. Excessive involvement in these activities may make him appear passionate, but they are only designed to avoid emotional entanglement.

For instance, Gerald, an architect, spent endless hours on projects that eventually earned him an excellent reputation. His dedication to creative design made him appear sensual and romantic, although his professional pursuits were used to avoid passion in his personal life. He spent long days at work and focused on goals that were irrelevant to his relationship with his fiancée. This frustrated her, and she began to long for social and emotional interaction.

(FIRST IMPRESSIONS)

When you first meet The Invisible Man, you may think he is quiet, distant, and perhaps even a little shy. His unshakable temperament makes him appear steady, unlike your last boyfriend. And you feel confident that eventually you will pull him out of his shell.

The Invisible Man will appear dedicated, confident, and impervious to disapproval. But these traits can be deceiving— and frustrating. Over time you begin to realize that The Invisible Man avoids recognition of what others think, and therefore may dress or act in a fashion that is embarrassing (his "good" shirts are the ones with the "clean" stains). This man can be oblivious to the subtleties of social interaction, and may need to be hit over the head in order to understand what you or others are saying. His lack of responsiveness gives the impression that he is aloof or uncaring. But the opposite is really true. Once The Invisible Man opens up, he is flooded with feeling. And it's this tendency toward being emotionally overwhelmed that made him shut down in the first place.

As with the other personalities in this book, The Invisible Man engages in a self-protective style that flavors his entire personality. His particular brand of self-protection involves denying personal emotions—emotions he fears could wound or destroy. But in his unconscious zeal to protect himself from psychological pain, he destroys the rich openness of feeling that makes life passionate and interesting.

[Jean's story]

Jean came to therapy to cope with a growing depression. She and her husband, Alex, had been married for three years.

Although he was dependable, he was also shut down and remote. Lately he seemed to be drifting further away.

Alex worked as a CPA. Every day he would faithfully go to work, come home, tend to the house, water the garden, and feed the dog. Despite his reliability, however, their lives were dull and uninteresting. Alex rarely agreed to go out, and he was reluctant to socialize with other couples.

Although they would go to a coffeehouse on Saturday mornings to spend time together, he would hold up the newspaper like an impenetrable barrier between them. Jean was discouraged, lonely, and tired of looking at newsprint (she also read faster than Alex, and he refused to turn the page).

As the name would suggest, The Invisible Man is frequently not present. For instance, he has an annoying tendency to drift away while you are talking. If you say, "Penny for your thoughts," or "Earth to so-and-so," he might *pretend* that he has been listening. He might even repeat what you have said, but just to appease you or to avoid a fight he'll remember only half a sentence. The Invisible Man is somewhat dishonest. Although he prefers to connect with inanimate objects and tasks, he knows that this is inappropriate and unacceptable. Therefore, he will pretend that he has been listening even when he has not.

When you inquire about this man's childhood, you may discover that he was raised by a volatile, intrusive, or demanding mother. And when you meet his mother, you realize that you, too, would have tried to become invisible in order to cope with this overbearing woman. You suggest surgery to have his mother removed from his back.

Whenever you ask The Invisible Man to emotionally show up and he cannot, you might want to ask yourself, *In his mind, have I become his mother? Is he warding off close personal interaction because he learned that this is what he must do in order to survive? Is it fruitful for me to be in a relationship where I am continually ignored?*

[Gaby's story]

When Gaby met Tim, she was struck by the compatibility of their interests. Tim had just bought a fixer-upper, and Gaby was interested in renovation and reconstruction. For the first two years of their relationship, they spent a great deal of time working on his house.

Flash-forward to a long-term marriage and a seven-year-old daughter. Gaby came to therapy with the complaint that Tim still spent every weekend working on their house. Gaby would ask Tim to go to a movie, but he was unable to break away from his spackling. Gaby would suggest a picnic at the beach, but Tim was too busy painting the sunroom. Weekends were spent with the sounds of drilling, sawing, and hammering.

And when Tim was not painting or spackling, he was playing riffs on his electric guitar. Other than his own interests, nothing excited him.

When Gaby finally dragged Tim to therapy, I noticed that he was a decent guy. But all of his energy was invested in the house, and there was nothing left over for Gaby or their child. I made the comment, "Tim, you seem more interested in the house than in Gaby. I wonder if it is safer to connect to a house than a person because a house cannot criticize you, demand more of you, or attempt to control you." Tim was initially resistant to my suggestion. But over time he agreed, and the therapy turned to helping him conquer his fear of deep interpersonal engagement.

The Invisible Man invests his passion in *inanimate objects* (houses, coin collections, cars, sports gear) and *impersonal pursuits* (hobbies, sports, travel, pets) because the further he drifts from his intimate relationships, the safer he feels. At an unconscious level he believes that while a woman might overwhelm or betray him, an inanimate object or impersonal pursuit will not.

Because of his love for the impersonal, however, The Invisible Man rarely adds anything new to a relationship. He rarely initiates, contributes, or enhances. Although he will spend twenty hours watching football, weather-stripping the windows, memorizing sports stats, or following the stock market, he will have no opinion when you ask where he wants to go to dinner. Do not—I repeat, *do not*—expect The Invisible Man to notice when you wear a sexy new outfit or change your hair color. He is not enlivened by the relationship, although he follows his own pursuits with meticulous detail.

The Invisible Man is constantly moving away from relationships, rather than toward them (although he likes the idea that you are waiting at home). Thus, he may prefer the mountains over the city. Travel over intimate dinners. Parasailing over holding hands. Trekking the Himalayas over planning for a mutually invested future.

The Invisible Man also detests conflict and would rather hop on the Internet than have a spirited debate. He avoids competitive relationships (even if he is at the top of his field, he is never in direct competition with anyone else). And when he finally becomes a father, he will swoop in and correct his children through harsh (and impersonal) disciplinary action. But he will rarely sit down and inquire about their feelings.

[Marie's story]

Marie brought her boyfriend to therapy because he could only fall asleep on the living room sofa while watching television. They had an active sex life, yet he rarely spent the night in her bed. The fact that he would loll on the couch yet refuse to cuddle up was a real deal breaker for Marie. After meeting her boyfriend, I realized that the true deal breaker was that he was an Invisible Man. He drifted from one hobby to another, yet rarely attended events that were important to Marie. He was quick to shut down discussions whenever they became contentious and was rarely interested in what others were expressing. He was agreeable to sex, but disconnected as soon as the sex act was over. He was home, yet never present.

(WARNING SIGNS)

This is what a relationship looks like with an Invisible Man:

You ask him questions— sometimes three times in a row.	He doesn't answer, pretends he doesn't hear you, or gives a vague response.
You throw a dinner party.	Although he helps, you feel that you must constantly direct him and tell him what to do.
You plan an outing with another couple.	He does not fully participate in the conversation. He acts as if he just met them. He dresses inappropriately.

You have fun at a party.	You look around, and he's not there. Although you want to stay longer, he is already waiting in the car.

(DAMAGED GOODS)

Mr. Damaged Goods is a small subcategory of The Invisible Man. He suffers from an inability to fully "show up" in an intimate relationship—but for more serious reasons. This wounded bird suffers from neurobiological syndromes such as depression, anxiety, and bipolar illness.

Whereas The Invisible Man avoids intimacy because he fears he will be overwhelmed, Mr. Damaged Goods avoids intimacy because he can't *help* but be overwhelmed. This man is suffering from a biologically based disorder for which he has not—or will not—seek help.

When you meet a man who has inexplicable mood swings—a man who is either shut down or hypersensitive . . . the type of guy who is overwhelmed by the normal demands of being in a relationship and the normal challenges of life—it would behoove you to think about whether or not he is anxious or depressed. The man who is psychiatrically challenged retreats from relationships—*but for reasons slightly different from those of the man described in the previous section.* Mr. Damaged Goods may be suffering from depression, anxiety, the effects of early trauma, mental illness in his extended family (even if he is not formally mentally ill, he may have shades of illness), substance abuse (as a form of self-medication), and/or interpersonal hypersensitivity (a so-called soft sign of bipolar disorder). In fact, women occasionally come to my office for relationship help only to discover that the true culprit is an undiagnosed mood disorder in their partner. Often they will notice a pattern of interpersonal hypersensitivity, a depressed or anxious mood, an inability to "connect the dots," or an altered perception of reality. They also observe a stubborn quality to his symptoms, even when he wants to feel better.

When this man is presented with a normal life stressor, such as a job demotion, the loss of a parent, or financial misfortune, watch out! He will not be able to cope and will fall apart.

[Megan's story]

Megan owned a flower shop and her husband was her driver. Megan began her business to help her husband, who was floundering. His only responsibility was to take orders and make deliveries. However, he sometimes wrote the orders incorrectly. And when Megan questioned him, he could not tell her what had gone wrong. Over time her business began to suffer. But the more she expressed her anger, the less capable he became.

In couples therapy, I noticed that he seemed extremely depressed. He hung his head, acted ashamed, and could not offer an adequate explanation as to why he was failing to pull his own weight. I did an assessment and discovered that he was experiencing sleep, appetite, and concentration disturbances—sure signs of depression. I referred him to a psychiatrist, who prescribed an antidepressant. Within a couple of months, his mood improved and he stopped making mistakes.

Megan was so resourceful and competent that she'd kept compensating for her husband's limitations. The more he failed, the more she'd redoubled her efforts. But once Megan realized that a good diagnosis is half of the cure and that depression is potentially curable through medication and therapy, she'd stopped rescuing him and encouraged him to seek the appropriate treatment.

The only way to know if he is clinically depressed, anxious, or suffering from bipolar illness is to refer him to a psychiatrist for a full evaluation. If he wants to get better, he will follow up with routine med checks, couples therapy, psychotherapy, twelve-step, a men's group, or whatever else is indicated. With professional help, there is a possibility that the relationship will spring back to life. If he refuses to get help or denies that he has a biologically based disorder, then his problem is a deal breaker and there is not much you can do.

Men who are depressed or anxious often tell me that although they want to be in a relationship, they find it difficult to be receptive and available. For instance, Joe, a middle-aged businessman, came to therapy because he wanted to find a girlfriend. In the first session, I learned that he had a history of panic attacks and that his anxiety worsened whenever he was in a relationship. I also learned that whenever Joe began a romance, he would drop out as soon as there was a minor problem. Here is what Joe said: "I want to be in a relationship, but I'm not sure that I can. When I'm on, I'm on. And when I'm not, I'm not. It's like a gear. When I'm in gear, everything moves forward. But when the gear slips out, everything goes off track."

Joe sought treatment, his anxiety dissipated, and he began to successfully date. But the only way that he was able to hold on to a relationship was to take full responsibility for his problem instead of taking it out on the woman in his life.

(WHO GOES THERE?)

I don't want to overwhelm you, but there's a third subcategory of The Invisible Man that you must watch out for! This is the man who purports to feel one way when, really, he feels another. Or who presents a false front, when underneath he has secret or unexpressed feelings and desires. Or who pretends to be enthusiastic when in fact he is not.

Have you dated a guy like that? He tells you he's straight, but you suspect that he is gay (especially when he tells you he's late for his brow wax)? He insists that he loves you, even though the last time he called, you were three pounds thinner? And when you tell him that you can tolerate the truth about how he feels, he insists that he is in love when in fact he isn't? What about the guy who is wonderful yet vacant? He takes you to dinner, holds open the door, pulls out your chair, pays the bill, but leaves you with the feeling that he wasn't really there. You know he wasn't connected, even though he did all the right things.

It is creepy to be in a relationship with someone whom you think you know, yet who is disingenuous or emotionally absent. Eventually you poke beneath the surface and discover that something else is lurking there.

[Tina's story]

Tina brought her fiancé to therapy because she had gone through one divorce and was determined to get this marriage right. Her fiancé showed up for every session, was respectful and polite, and even offered suggestions for her bridal dress and bouquet. But when it came to deeper issues (such as *his* joy and thoughts of commitment), he was vague and uncertain. For instance, he had proposed in a splashy and dramatic way in front of all her friends (he flashed the words "Will You Marry Me?" on a movie screen during a party). When I asked him about this, he revealed that Tina had placed great pressure upon him to make the proposal special. Yet when I asked him if he had enjoyed proposing marriage, he was unable to tell me how he felt. He said, "It was okay," but not, "It gave me great pleasure to propose marriage to Tina." He was polite, yet somehow removed.

Whenever I explored his hopes and dreams for the future, he actually parroted Tina's words and phrases! He never came up with his own thoughts, only reflections of hers.

Unlike the kind of Invisible Man who is afraid to connect and contents himself with impersonal activities and pursuits, this pretender *appears* to connect—yet never owns up to his true thoughts, secret ambitions, and fervently held beliefs. This man can be very confusing, because he does all the right things. He goes to church, plans the wedding, raises the children, and so on. But there is a tentativeness to every enterprise, and you are left wondering if he really wants to be there in the first place.

For instance, David sought therapy to cope with a painful divorce. In therapy, he disclosed that he had married his wife because his parents liked her. During the course of their marriage, he bought a cute cottage, had two children, and worked in an art gallery in order to meet his financial obligations. When David fell into a depression, his family insisted that he go to therapy. Over time (and I had to drag it out of him), I learned not only that David had married his wife primarily because his family had bonded with her, but also that, although he adored his children, he was ambivalent about being a father. His secret ambition was to be an artist, so it was torturous for him to work in a gallery that represented artists following their dreams when he had failed to follow his. Within a few months David shamefully confessed that he had developed an online porn addiction. I thought, *No wonder! It is probably the only excitement in your drab, empty existence. Given your personality, I am not surprised that the one exciting pursuit in your life is carried out in secret!*

This subcategory of The Invisible Man is so intent on pleasing everybody that he pleases nobody—not even himself. And he is so intent on avoiding disapproval that he presents a squeaky-clean exterior that belies the internal void he has created. Often, his relationships end with the disastrous discovery that he is not really in love, that he secretly resents his partner, that he has hidden sexual interests, or that he is obsessed with a secret emotional life about which nobody has been aware.

Girlfriend—if he says he is unsure about being in a relationship, *listen to him*! If he says he must have an alternative sexual lifestyle in order to be happy, *do not attempt to dissuade him*. If he wants a divorce, *do not drag him to marital counseling against his will.* If he has thoughts about traveling abroad and exploring the world on his own, *pay attention to what he is telling you!* If he says he is unhappy, and you can read the writing on the wall, *run—don't walk—away from the relationship!*

Remember the deal breaker cheat sheet? You can't work harder than he does to resolve his problems or work out issues in the relationship. And good relationships are equally and mutually invested in. If something is not working, it is okay to walk away and to admit that it was never meant to be.

Once you discover that he cannot form a deep attachment, that the slightest conflict makes him retreat behind an impenetrable wall, that covering up feelings is more important than relating to you, and that you are responsible for all the intimacy in the relationship—you know that it is a deal breaker rather than a minor problem.

(WHO CHOOSES THIS TYPE OF MAN?)

If you find yourself wishing, hoping, and praying for more intimacy with an Invisible Man, perhaps you were raised by parents who made you feel that you had to accept relationship tidbits rather than wholehearted devotion. Perhaps when you asked for more, your parents made you feel greedy. And when you turned to them for help, you were handed a slim excuse rather than a hearty solution. Thus, you came to feel that it was all up to you to take care of yourself. And you repeated this dynamic when you chose an Invisible Man who made you feel that you had to fall back on your own resources instead of turning to him for help and understanding.

Megan, the woman who owned a flower shop, was raised by a mother who worked the graveyard shift at a convenience store, did not make enough money to buy her daughter new clothes, and spent the afternoons sleeping. As an adolescent Megan earned her own money, cooked her own meals, and hitched rides to school and other extracurricular activities. Because she had learned to scrap for herself as a child, she did not notice when she began scrapping for her needs in her primary love relationship. And because she had become so talented at reaching for her own solutions, she barely noticed when her husband did not help her. Megan later discovered that her mother had been severely depressed yet had never sought treatment—just like Megan's husband.

Marie, the woman whose husband would not sleep in her bed, was raised by highly competent parents. Her father was a politician, and her mother was an attorney who helped the inner-city poor. But both parents prioritized the needs of others over the needs of their own children. Marie's father missed his daughter's high school recitals in order to work on congressional bills. And Marie's mother donated time and money to the poor while her daughter was still young, with needs of her own. Because Marie had been made to feel that others were more important than she was, she barely noticed when her husband began gravitating toward his hobbies and away from their relationship.

Because Megan and Marie felt invisible throughout childhood, they tolerated relationships that were depriving and empty. And because they were raised by parents who were not completely available, they learned to make excuses for bad behavior:

"He didn't really mean that."

"He's busy supporting me—that's why he's so uncommunicative."

"I'm asking for too much."

"I must have done something to upset him."

"But he's so brilliant, I should let him devote himself to his career (hobbies, other interests, et cetera)."

It was not until Megan and Marie woke up and realized that that they were doing all the work that they were finally able to free themselves from the trap their parents had set for them. Once their hearts and minds connected, they realized that their thoughts had been all wrong. Instead of repeating the platitude "Don't be discouraged—it will soon be much better," they were able to tell themselves: He *is the one who is disconnected. He is the one with the problem. He is the one who needs to make the effort.*

Stepping back from the endless process of fluffing up the

relationship, the decision to leave was easy—because there was no emotional glue holding the relationship together.

(WHEN IS IT A DEAL BREAKER?)

If it is a deal breaker, you will begin to notice that most conversations with The Invisible Man do not lead to anything new. In fact, you may find yourself repeating the same words and phrases that you have used so many times before! Yet there are no new connections, no new insights, no new plans, no new goals, no new ways of being, no new patterns—and never a new direction in the relationship.

DEAL BREAKER SCENARIO: He watches sports (hunts, fishes, exercises, follows the stock market, works on projects, surfs the Internet) all day. He refuses to break away from his precious interests in order to spend time together. When the wall is up, it won't come down. You feel a deeper connection with the phone survey guy than you do with him.

WORK ON IT: You ask him to let go of his obsessive behavior and he begins to work on it. You see signs of movement and evidence of change. Perhaps he designates an area of your lives in which both of you are mutually invested, such as going to the gym together, taking a cooking class, or planning vacations. His willingness to connect gives you hope and something to hold on to—not the wishing, hoping, and praying kind of hope, but something genuine and real.

WALK AWAY: You, and only you, are interested in a deeper emotional engagement. Whenever you ask for more, you feel as if you are banging your head against the wall. In the end, you realize that you are living your life without a companion. With sadness, you realize that when there is nothing shared, it is not really a relationship.

DEAL BREAKER SCENARIO: When you first met, he was sexually attracted to you. You couldn't even undress without his becoming excited. But now you parade around the bedroom in lingerie, yet he cannot break away from the television (a new flat-screen? Now, *that* excites him). And you cuddle next to him in bed, but he refuses to respond. Because he remains detached, you feel like less of a woman.

WORK ON IT: You tell him that you need the reassurance that he is sexually interested, and you back up your request by buying sexy lingerie, planning a romantic getaway, or trying different things. Because you have made an effort, he begins to desire you and initiate sex. The renewed sexuality "warms up" the relationship in other areas.

WALK AWAY: He doesn't respond, gives no explanation as to why he is sexually disinterested, refuses to talk about it, and remains detached. No matter what you try, his sexual interest is not revived. Whereas a *King of Queens* rerun used to be more important than sex, a *Teletubbies* rerun is now more important than sex.

DEAL BREAKER SCENARIO: You suspect that he is somebody other than whom you thought he was. For instance, he keeps you separated from a group of friends who know everything about him. Or he tells you that he despises bars, but spends an evening at a bar while you are out of town. Or you discover that he has been chatting with an online community about a weird sexual fetish. You wonder, *Who is this man?*

WORK ON IT: When you bring it to his attention, he offers a reasonable explanation and takes ownership of his behavior. He tells you that his friends are big drinkers and he has been embarrassed to introduce you to them. Or that he went to the bar to accommodate a business client. Or that even though he is slightly interested in the fetish, he is more interested in being in a wholesome relationship with you.

When you tell him how you feel, he responds to your concern. He invites you out with his friends or tells you more about the part of his life that he has been hiding. In the end, you discover that his secret is not antithetical to being in a full relationship.

WALK AWAY: When you tell him how you feel, he calls you hypersensitive. He disavows the fact that he has been hiding something from you. The discrepancy between who he presents himself as being and who he really is becomes a chronic problem.

DEAL BREAKER SCENARIO: He refuses to go out with your friends. Although you long for social interaction with the outside world, he does nothing to facilitate it. When you invite him to attend a cocktail party, he sits in the corner and offers little. He is a lump on a log with your extended family, too.

WORK ON IT: Although it may be difficult for him to understand, you explain to him what it is like to fully participate in the life of your family and friends. To your pleasant surprise, he begins to show an interest in them and talk with them about himself.

WALK AWAY: Instead of going out with your friends, he talks about building a crawl space. He uses every excuse in the book for why he should not socialize with them. Even when he makes an attempt, he is unable to connect. With disappointment, you realize that his social chip is missing and that you cannot replace it.

(IF YOU SUSPECT HE IS AN INVISIBLE MAN)

The only way to know if you should work on a relationship with The Invisible Man is to notice whether he can make a reciprocal effort. For instance, you reach out your hand and he reaches back. You ask for a connection and he folds you in his embrace. You put some elbow grease into the relationship and he begins to respond. You ask him to come clean and he offers a clear and understandable explanation.

But if you want him more than he wants you . . . if you redouble your efforts to compensate for his disinterest . . . if you invest your valuable time in order to facilitate his false impressions . . . then it is time to walk away.

A colleague of mine once quipped, "In relationships, we all pick our poison." I quickly replied, "Yes—but we shouldn't be so tolerant, reasonable, and open-minded that our brains fall out of our heads. Sometimes a concerted effort to be fair and accommodating can be a sophisticated form of denying that the relationship is not really working." (Okay, her quote is pithier—but my quote could change your life.)

The Little Boy Who Poses as a Man

The Little Boy Who Poses as a Man will not fully reciprocate or take complete responsibility for himself because he finds it easier to remain childlike and needy.

It is four o'clock on a Thursday afternoon, and Kelly is telling me about her relationship with her boyfriend, Greg. "I thought our relationship was going well. The other night, I took Greg out to dinner and dancing. The food was great. The sex was even better. But it's been three days and he hasn't called me. Am I doing something wrong? It seems that we only get together when I make all the plans or do the calling."

Has this ever happened to you? Your boyfriend is willing and enthusiastic as long as you do all the initiating and planning, but as soon as you step back because it is his turn to reciprocate, he drifts away instead of moving closer?

Kelly was soon to find out that she *was* making a mistake

127

and had unwittingly chosen a man who looked more grown-up than he really was. And as is the way with these types of men, Greg was getting Kelly to act like a "mommy" and take all the responsibility for the relationship.

(FIRST IMPRESSIONS)

The Little Boy Who Poses as a Man is easy to fall in love with because he needs you. But he brings hard work and frustration when it comes to making a commitment and building a fulfilling life together.

At the beginning it is interesting and amusing to be with a man who is fun and exciting. The Little Boy Who Poses as a Man breaks down inhibitions and reinvigorates the dull routine of adult life. He is primarily pleasure seeking, and always enthusiastic about having a good time. For example, he may be a bad boy who shrugs off obligations.

But The Little Boy Who Poses as a Man is *only* capable of childlike excitement (and when you tell him that opening a strip club at Disneyland is not a sound idea, he fails to see your point). He never progresses to other important and necessary aspects of mature adult life, such as commitment, responsibility, reciprocity, and emotional growth—the ingredients you need for a healthy, happy, and wholesome life.

The Little Boy Who Poses as a Man is reluctant to grow

up, because at some point during his childhood it became more comfortable to remain childlike. As you know, children retain many privileges. They are taken care of, protected, provided for, and loved despite their many faults. They don't even have to work for a living or take responsibility for themselves!

The Little Boy Who Poses as a Man clings to these childhood privileges and feels entitled to having his needs met without personal effort or reciprocity. For example, he may expect a relationship to run smoothly without communication or personal investment. Or he may expect to be taken care of and nurtured without giving the same in return (he may not get the whole "taxes thing"). Sometimes, he will want his life planned without having to personally concentrate on the larger picture. In more severe cases, he will refuse to get a job or succeed at the level of his true capabilities.

[Jenna's story]

Jenna met her boyfriend, Jay, while working at a law firm. He was an attorney, and she was the office manager. Jenna was ambitious and eventually left the law practice to begin her own consulting firm. Much to Jay's disappointment, her business required travel and business dinners with clients.

Although Jenna's business prospered, her relationship did

not. Jay became irritable and withholding whenever she traveled. And he eventually refused to accompany her to business dinners, claiming that he was tired of watching her "fawn" over her clients. Despite the fact that Jenna was reaching for her own happiness and fulfilling her goals, Jay refused to support her professional endeavors. Frustrated, Jenna finally asked, "Why is it so difficult for you to support me in my profession?" Jay responded, "Because this is not what I signed up for!"

Jenna had entered the relationship without realizing that she was dating a Little Boy. Thus, she failed to realize that the unconsciously agreed-upon relationship arrangement was that of a mother devoting herself to a child. And as is expected when a mother takes care of a child, "mommy" is supposed to do all the giving, while "little boy" does all the taking. Furthermore, "mommy" is supposed to supply time, love, and endless adoration, while "little boy" remains the sole recipient of her attention.

(WARNING SIGNS)

Here's what happens when you spend time with a Little Boy who wants to be taken care of without offering anything in return:

You are a go-getter.	He thinks a go-getter is someone who goes and gets him a beer.
You have a life.	When he talks about his place and his parents' home, you have a sneaking suspicion that they may be the same place.
You engage in an ongoing sexual relationship with him.	Initially he seems interested and engaged. But over time his interest is not backed up by action. When you ask yourself, *What has this man given me?* you realize that he has added little to your life.
You spend months or years with him.	He does not offer a marital commitment (little boys aren't supposed to marry their mothers). You give and he takes.
You earn money.	He spends it or refuses to adequately produce resources of his own.
You labor and sweat to make both your lives better.	He believes that things come easily to you.
You invest emotionally.	He easily walks away from the relationship, as if you have done little to help him and the relationship does not hold much meaning. In hindsight, you realize that he never gave your feelings much thought.

Simply put, a mother takes care of her child without expecting anything in return. And the gift of the child's love is considered sufficient reward for her considerable investment. Yet when a grown man asks, "Isn't my love enough to make you happy?" the appropriate response is no. As I mentioned earlier, all good relationships are based upon mutual give and take. And in healthy relationships, *both* parties benefit equally from the arrangement.

(HOW TO KNOW IF HE'S A LITTLE BOY WHO POSES AS A MAN)

Does he track your every movement? Or cling to you? Do you feel like you cannot leave him alone for long periods of time?

Is your man like that? He latches on or imagines that you are not invested in the relationship? Or he feels that if you are out of sight, *he* is out of mind? Perhaps he does not trust that you are there for him. Or he feels that if the two of you are temporarily separated, he will fall apart.

For example, you initiate a girls' night out, and he becomes convinced that you are going to forget about him and flirt with other guys (which, of course, makes you want to forget about him and flirt with other guys). So he calls you all night long to remind you that he still exists. And when you come home, he questions you and punishes you for staying out so long. In extreme cases, he threatens to end the relationship if you continue to spend significant amounts of time away from him.

If you feel like a mommy, and if he cannot control his anxiety when the two of you are apart, then you have a deal breaker on your hands. And if you are a reliable girlfriend, yet he feels that he must dominate or possess you so that you don't slip away, he needs to grow up and leave his inner child at the door!

[Lucia's story]

Lucia met Andrew on a blind date. Lucia had many friendships and a full life. Andrew was adventurous and loved to hike and surf. Their passion for life ignited a quick romance.

Within a few months, however, Lucia noticed that Andrew had difficulty being left alone for any significant amount of time. Whenever they were separated, he would question her about her plans or make suggestions about time management. If she decided to go to yoga, he would offer to meet her for dinner immediately following the class. Over time the questioning escalated to whether or not she really needed to go to yoga. In the final stages of "dominate and control" he began to accuse her of squandering the precious time that they had together.

Whenever Lucia tried to set up inclusive social plans,

Andrew would refuse to attend. Yet whenever she went out with friends, he was upset and felt left out. By the time Lucia came to therapy, she was overwhelmed because she had no time for herself and little contact with friends.

As is typical with infantile men, Andrew did not trust Lucia to naturally be invested in him or the relationship. And he feared that without his constant reminders, she would not devote herself to him.

This is what it is like to be with a man who feels that it is all up to him to hold on to you:

You go shopping with girlfriends.	He asks you multiple times about when you will return. When you leave the house, the dog whines less than he does.
You come home a half hour late because you were stuck in traffic.	He is distressed because you didn't call him. When you offer a reasonable explanation, he refuses to understand. You feel horrible because he makes you believe that you did something wrong.
You ask him to go out with you and your friends.	He won't hang out with them, but he's sure they're a bad influence.

You find a new job.	He questions you about whom you met on the first day of the job.
You go away for the weekend.	Instead of entertaining himself, he addictively turns to substitute "mommies," such as food, computer games, online porn, or anything else that will numb or comfort him.

The Little Boy Who Poses as a Man is possessive for a variety of reasons. In some cases, he is anxious and cannot stand to be left alone. In other cases, he confuses momentary separation with abandonment. Like a small child, he may demand continual proof that he is loved (draw the line at breast feeding). Or he may feel safer when he is in your presence. On the other hand, he may simply be having a hard time because he used up all the prepaid minutes that you bought for him to check up on you.

[Dolly's story]

Dolly came to therapy because she and her boyfriend, Gilbert, were fighting over how much time to spend together and how much time to spend apart. They had been dating for three months and had rarely left each other's side. And Dolly needed to catch up on her e-mails, call her friends, go to the gym, and get a little time for herself. But when she told Gilbert that she needed an afternoon alone, he began to make hostile comments. "I guess you like your friends better than me." "I wish you would have given me advance warning so that I could have planned my weekend." When Dolly turned to her friends for support, Gilbert commented, "It must be nice to have friends to tell you what to do."

Gilbert's reluctance to give Dolly personal space made her feel overwhelmed and confused. In therapy I helped Dolly understand that Gilbert was a little boy who refused to grow up. And as is the case with children, he had a difficult time discerning the difference between temporary separation and outright abandonment. Whenever he and Dolly were apart, he viewed her as a mommy who was hurtfully abandoning him rather than as a girlfriend who had her own separate schedule and needs. Thus, he could not discern the difference between "me time" and personal rejection.

Once Dolly understood that the problem stemmed from Gilbert's childhood experiences and not from her, she was able to be more assertive and talk to him openly. Gilbert was then forced to work on his feelings instead of blaming his anxiety on her.

Afraid you have a deal breaker on your hands? Put him to the separation stress test. Tell him you are taking a hiatus from answering the cell phone each and every time he calls. Better yet, tell him that you are going out of town with your girl-friends. If he allows you to go without guilt or recrimination, and holds himself together while you are gone, then he is a keeper and your relationship has a chance.

If he throws himself on the floor and has a temper tan-trum, keep reading.

(LITMUS TEST)

Is he a patchwork of ideas and emotions that do not go together? For instance, he claims to be morally superior yet says things that are petty and mean? Or he acts dependent and needy but cheats on you as soon as your back is turned?

Once again, let's consider the mind of the child. When a small child falls down, he begins to cry. Yet the minute you dust him off and cheer him up, he will forget about the painful feelings that afflicted him just moments before. In fact, he will probably run off to play, giving no thought to the fact that he might fall down and once again hurt himself.

Immature men, like small children, also switch quickly from one emotion to another with little memory of what they just felt, said, or did. Or of what the two of you just experienced together.

[Don's story]

Don was set up on a date by mutual friends. At the last minute, his date canceled with the thin excuse that she needed to take care of her sick mother. Because Don knew that his reluctant dinner companion worked at a local restaurant, he decided to go there for dinner and prove that she was lying and was really working. At the same time, he rationalized to himself that *he* was a reliable guy who would never have mistreated another human being by canceling at the last minute. And most certainly, *he* would never have lied! Don's idea that he was superior existed alongside the idea that his date should be exposed and punished. See what I mean? The idea *I am a good person* does not match up with the idea *I am going to punish you in a mean-spirited way*! Don quickly shifted from hopefulness about the date to hatefulness in the wake of his own disappointment. His emotions fluctuated so wildly that he never even considered that his date might have decided to work because she needed the money. Or that she might not have been able to get somebody to take over her shift but was too embarrassed to tell him.

This is the litmus test: Like a child, he cannot hold on to good feelings when confronted by painful situations. For instance, he claims to love you but overreacts when he is disappointed. Or he tells you that he adores you but punishes you viciously if you forget to call. Perhaps he is in an extraordinarily good mood but flips into a rage when he is cut off by another vehicle on the way to dinner (because it reminds him of a time that he felt cut off by you). Here are more examples:

• He tells you that he understands you but withdraws or sulks if you disagree with him.

• He asks you to set aside time to help him with appointments and errands but then accuses you of being too dependent upon him.

• He feels that you should accompany him everywhere but fails to introduce you to his friends at the work holiday party.

• He acts dependent and needy but flirts with girls as soon as your back is turned.

If your man believes that you should be continually maternally available, he will corner you into taking total responsibility for him. But if you do not give perfectly (or fail to read his mind), then your separateness will be interpreted as a betrayal. When you are devoted, he will perceive you as "all good." But when you disappoint him or let him down, he will experience you as "all bad." On a particularly bad day you may be tempted to escape into the Witness Protection Program just for the hell of it.

[Elizabeth's story]

Elizabeth moved in with Alex after six months of dating. Their love affair had been tempestuous, and they frequently fought over how much time each was allowed to spend with friends. After Elizabeth moved in, she rarely left Alex's side except to go to work or run minor errands. One night Elizabeth's friends asked her to go out with them. Despite Alex's protestations, she agreed. While she was gone, Alex became convinced that other men had been invited and that he had been excluded. He also became worried that Elizabeth might be rendezvousing with an old lover. He became angry and began to serial dial her cell phone. When he could not reach her, he began to search her purses and pockets for phone numbers. Then he rifled through her jewelry box, convinced that she was saving trinkets from old boyfriends. By the time Elizabeth returned home, Alex had convinced himself that she was a thoughtless, selfish, cheating, lying philanderer who had never truly been invested in him. He adhered to this belief even when Elizabeth reminded him that she had made a huge sacrifice to leave her former life and move in with him.

In the contradictory mind of The Little Boy, there is often a thin line between love and hate, trust and mistrust, good feelings and bad feelings. Alex was enamored of Elizabeth as long as she focused her attentions solely upon him. At the first hint of separateness, she became all bad and no longer possessed any positive qualities.

Afraid you have a similar deal breaker on your hands? Put him to the conversation test. Tell him you have noticed that some of his thoughts and actions seem contradictory. Point out the vast discrepancy between what he said yesterday and how he is behaving today. Or comment upon the fact that he seemed so adoring last week, yet now believes that you are a horrible or disappointing person. If he is an overgrown child, he may pout, fuss, become suspicious, or refuse to think about what is happening to him. But if he is capable of growing up and developing new understandings about you, a somewhat thoughtful discussion should ensue about his inability to manage his own painful feelings.

(WHO CHOOSES THIS TYPE OF MAN?)

Perhaps you were drawn to The Little Boy because you were looking for a good time. Little boys are energetic and playful, and promise to infuse a relationship with youthfulness and fun. Besides, little boys are cute even when they are being tremendously selfish (so naughty!).

If you choose men who crave lots of love and attention—men who cannot grow up and take appropriate responsibility for themselves—perhaps you are attracted to regressed personalities.

Perhaps you are a nurturer, and thrive on the experience of being wanted and needed. Over time, however, you begin to realize that your efforts are not being reciprocated. And your relationship begins to feel tedious, imbalanced, and unfair.

In the final phase of your relationship you begin to feel guilty for harboring thoughts about abandoning your under-functioning partner. You begin to realize that without you, he may not thrive. But as you consider moving from nurturer to disappointer, you begin to fear that he may withdraw his love. So you redouble your efforts in order to keep him afloat. As you do this, however, you begin to grow him down instead of growing him up. And the more he relies upon you, the more difficult it is for you to leave. The twin fears that he will flounder and that you will be abandoned become the glue that holds the dysfunctional relationship together.

Over time, you begin to suppress your needs in order to hold on to the love that you so desperately want. And finally, you develop the paralyzing fear that if you leave, he may improve on his own and give *some other girl* the new and improved version of him that you have wanted for so long.

(WHEN IS IT A DEAL BREAKER?)

Many of the personality problems that erupt into deal breakers are holdovers from the earliest parts of life. It is important to note that every personality (yours included) is mildly infused with the qualities and characteristics of childhood. But when a boyfriend or husband cannot make a meaningful relationship contribution and resists appropriate experiences of separating and then coming back together—then the little boy is stronger than the man.

DEAL BREAKER SCENARIO: He won't spend time with your family.

WORK ON IT: He won't spend time with them because they are obnoxious (you don't really want to spend time with them either). When you discuss the problem with him, however, he addresses his reluctance yet still makes a plan to see them occasionally.

WALK AWAY: He refuses to spend time with your family because he is a self-involved child who wants to watch sports games, drink beer, go four-wheeling, or work on his projects instead of involving himself in your life. Or he refuses to spend time with them because he wants you all to himself. Despite your unhappiness, he refuses to modify his behavior.

DEAL BREAKER SCENARIO: He refuses to ask for a promotion, advance himself in his career, or make enough money to support himself and/or the family. With a sinking feeling, you realize that he is not ambitious.

WORK ON IT: He is doing the best he can, but there are no opportunities available. And if there are, he is willing to ask for help and understands his roadblocks.

WALK AWAY: He passively gets by because he has a history of being taken care of by others. Or he simply lacks ambition and is content with a modest lifestyle. You work harder than he does to improve his professional opportunities because he feels that it is a tragedy to work.

On the other hand, perhaps you made a deal at the beginning of the relationship that he could not adhere to. You envisioned him as a business mogul when in fact he was happy with his less lucrative profession. Or you imagined that he would someday strike it rich, yet failed to let him in on your true ambitions. If you discover that the mistake was yours, it is still okay to walk away.

DEAL BREAKER SCENARIO: He dresses badly and has poor grooming habits. When he smiles, you cannot take your eyes off his bad teeth (God invented dental plans for a reason). With a sinking heart, you realize that he is not invested in taking care of himself.

WORK ON IT: He has bad teeth and raggedy clothing because no one *taught* him to take care of himself. At your suggestion (and with your help), he books a dental appointment and goes shopping. He does this because he is grateful for the chance to improve himself and wants to fit in with his peers. (Note: I said, "He is grateful for the chance to improve himself," not "He is a pushover who submits to a makeover simply to make you happy.")

WALK AWAY: He does not groom himself because he is a Little Boy who thinks he is adorable no matter what he does, how he dresses, how bad he smells, or how rotten his teeth are. Or he cannot see himself accurately and therefore does not care how he comes across to others. Thus, he is out of sync with society. Although you are bothered by his appearance, he remains unconcerned. And his degenerating appearance is reflected in multiple other areas of his life, which are also disintegrating.

DEAL BREAKER SCENARIO: He won't propose marriage and refuses to talk about the future.

WORK ON IT: He won't propose marriage because you are still getting to know each other and he is not yet prepared to take the next step. However, he discusses his reservations in such a way that they are fully comprehensible to you (even though you may not like them). Despite his unwillingness to marry, there is a future-mindedness to the relationship. Thus, he continues to make plans and the relationship is always moving forward.

WALK AWAY: He won't propose marriage because, like a child, he expects you to devote yourself to him without a reciprocal commitment. He refuses to talk about the future. He won't even share his thoughts about what might happen in the next year. When you ask him about his intentions, he blows up or says something obtuse like, "Why would I be with you if I didn't love you?" "We live as though we are married. . . . I don't understand why you are upset!" "Aren't I just with you?" You suspect that he is not as invested in you as you are in him.

DEAL BREAKER SCENARIO: He does not plan financially for the future, nor does he feel he has to. Although he has some savings, he never imagines having to provide for anyone other than himself (even his future children).

WORK ON IT: When you broach the subject, he can see that he has been thinking only of himself. He also recognizes that this would never work in a long-term relationship. He sits down with a financial planner at your request.

WALK AWAY: He does not plan financially for the future because he functions beneath the level of his true capacities or unconsciously holds out hope of being taken care of by you. When you ask him about his financial plans, he becomes angry and prevents a discussion. He believes that the future will magically take care of itself.

DEAL BREAKER SCENARIO: He punishes you whenever he is upset. He does this through withholding sex or affection, threatening to leave, using the children as pawns, attacking your reputation, questioning your devotion, accusing you of being immoral, becoming angry . . .

WORK ON IT: I hate to break it to you, but punishment is never an appropriate solution to interpersonal conflict (but yes, it does make us feel better). Small children punish because they have not yet found the appropriate words to communicate their disapproval (they do not know how to say, "I was afraid that you forgot about me"). Adults, on the other hand, should know how to appropriately assert themselves whenever they feel threatened or upset.

When you tell him that he has been immature, however, he acknowledges the inappropriateness of his actions and works on it without continual reminders. Thus, he demonstrates a willingness to change.

WALK AWAY: He punishes you because he has learned to bully rather than to express himself through meaningful dialogue. He knows that when he withdraws, shouts, becomes mean, or discredits you, he prevents you from sharing your feelings or disagreeing with him. When you point this out, he refuses to listen, and the relationship hits a brick wall. Upon reflection, you realize that there's room for only one bully in your life and that's your mother.

DEAL BREAKER SCENARIO: He constantly flirts with other women (women not nearly as hot as you, of course). You catch him checking out other women when the two of you are together.

WORK ON IT: He is a charismatic person who loves others and loves life. Although he enjoys women, he is firmly committed to you. He never flirts behind your back, because he is not deceptive. And when you tell him you feel threatened, *he responds by changing his behavior.* He understands the difference between impulse and action. Therefore, he looks at women because they are beautiful, not because he is undressing them in his mind.

WALK AWAY: Although you tell him that his flirtations are upsetting, *he flagrantly continues to ignore your feelings.* He is unable to comprehend that you feel insecure or threatened. You suspect that he is an emotional or sexual junkie, going from one gratifying experience to another. You also realize that he begins rubbernecking whenever things get rough in the relationship.

DEAL BREAKER SCENARIO: He feels jealous and out of control, and he blames the problem on you.

WORK ON IT: When you talk about the problem, he begins to take responsibility for his insecurities instead of taking them out on you.

WALK AWAY: He is so jealous that he asks you to terminate valuable friendships and relationships. Although you insert reality by letting him know that he is important, he is not reassured and cannot observe that he is being irrational. With a sinking feeling, you realize that outsiders are considered interlopers. Worst yet, he feels that he must be the *only person* in your life in order to be the *most important person* in your life.

DEAL BREAKER SCENARIO: He won't help around the house unless you continually remind him.

WORK ON IT: When you tell him that you feel overworked, he makes concessions or begins to pitch in without repeated reminders. Or he contributes in other ways, such as earning a good living or taking care of the children.

WALK AWAY: The last time he helped around the house, your roots weren't showing and the vodka bottle in your freezer was still full. Because he is a poster child for deferred adulthood, you nag, nag, nag, while he waits for instructions.

(IF YOU SUSPECT HE IS A LITTLE BOY WHO POSES AS A MAN)

The best way to determine if you should work on it or walk away is to treat him like a responsible adult. If you hold him to the same standards that apply to other mature human beings, then you will easily discover if his problem is a deal breaker or a minor concern.

The best way to treat him like a grown-up is to say:

"Honey, I have been noticing that you don't seem concerned about meeting my needs" (follow with an example).

"Babe, I have been noticing that something bad happens whenever we spend a little time apart."

"Sweetheart, I notice that I am doing all the work and that I am the only one who is concerned about the future."

"Darling, sometimes you think I am a bad person who does not have your best interests at heart."

Hopefully, these comments will get him to talk about the relationship or think about his behavior. If he rationalizes his behavior, becomes angry, or walks out of the room, then I do not hold out much hope for your relationship. If he uses your comments as an opportunity for good, productive dialogue that leads to real change (translation: He takes action on the things that are upsetting you), then you have a fighting chance.

It is important to note that The Little Boy Who Poses as a Man will often take what I call a "flight into health" when confronted with problems or threatened with a breakup. In other words, he might run to therapy, propose marriage, start giving gifts, or accompany you to dinner with your friends. But change is not genuine unless it continues unprompted and persists over time. If he asks you to *remind* him to go to therapy, to assist him in getting a job, to curtail your friendships so that he won't become jealous, or look up AA meetings so that he can get sober, then don't be fooled into thinking he has changed!

Let me spell it out:

DEAL BREAKER SCENARIO: He refuses to grow up. This is reflected in his unwillingness to control himself or to appropriately achieve in many areas of his life. The relationship is hard work for you and a breeze for him.

WORK ON IT: He accepts responsibility for his behavior, gets help for the problem *without overdependence upon your assistance,* and continues to improve with "no strings attached" (without the promise that if he changes the relationship will continue). In every conversation, you feel that he is continuing to work on the problem rather than entrenching his position.

WALK AWAY: He refuses to change or blames his problem on you. Or he only agrees to change if you promise to reunite with him. Or he tells you that he will mend his ways, but you end up prompting and reminding in order to keep him on track. You realize that if the relationship ends, he will quickly revert to his old self.

Women who walk away from a relationship with a Little Boy because of an unresolved deal breaker often come to my office with the following observation: "I did so much for him through-out the course of our relationship. And for years he made me believe that he could not survive without me! But when I finally asked him to meet *my* needs, he made me feel that it was my responsibility to help him change. And when I told him that it was too much work to take that responsibility on as well, he walked away from the relationship as if it meant nothing to him!"

I usually reply, "Of course! The less he invests in a relation-ship, the easier it is for him to leave. And it is always easier to leave an object that serves a function than to separate from an individual who is valuable in her own right. Besides, little boys are supposed to grow up and leave their mothers."

What Should I Do Now?

You've read about the five deal-breaking personality styles, and now you're thinking, *My God, what have I gotten myself into?* Or, *I can't believe that my man-hating girlfriend was right!* (Substitute: *My mother was right.*) Or, *At any moment he's going to morph into the Monster-I-Knew-He-Was-All-Along.*

Take a deep breath and *relax.*

One of the most frightening memories I have of graduate school was reading something called the *Diagnostic and Statistical Manual of Mental Disorders.* This illuminating little book contains every deal-breaking personality disorder and psychiatric syndrome that can afflict a person (leave it on your coffee table and terrify your dates). When my professor asked our class to read the book, each student came back the next week with the gripping worry that his or her loved one was possessed with all the psychological illnesses that the book described.

It was not until I had completed two doctorates and spent nineteen years in private clinical practice that I learned an important lesson about deal-breaking personality styles: It is not just an individual's personality type that determines whether or not his problem is a deal breaker. It is 1) whether or not he has the capacity to observe himself realistically, and 2) whether or not he wants to change.

If your boyfriend or husband understands that he has a problem, observes how he comes across to others, and realizes that he is damaging his relationships and his life, then there's hope! If he feels that everybody is to blame but him, it is a true deal breaker and there is nothing you can do to help him (even if he stays in therapy for a decade).

[Julie's story]

Julie came to therapy because she was in relationship hell. Her boyfriend, Charles, was paranoid about being ignored and had recently coerced her into moving in with him. He was also very possessive and poisoned all her friendships by saying terrible things behind her back. The night before Julie came to my office, Charles picked a fight, asked her to drive them home, pulled the hand brake while she was driving eighty miles an hour down the freeway, and spun out her car—almost killing them.

After telling me this story, Julie looked at me and said, "Do you think he can change? Or is this just in his DNA? I keep asking him to control his temper, but he never does. I've even made lists of what he needs to do. He agrees to follow it, but months pass and nothing changes."

Julie was reluctant to acknowledge the true deal breaker—that Charles did not want to change. Charles *liked* to pick fights. And Charles found it deeply satisfying to be angry and out of control. Furthermore, Charles was successful every time he manipulated Julie, and therefore he had no motivation to improve his behavior.

Unless a man's symptoms are painful to him, he will not change. And unless he can reflect upon his problem, he will never improve. If a man's deal-breaking personality problem feels good to him, there is nothing you can do about it.

(FOR EVERY PROBLEM, THERE IS A SOLUTION)

At this point, you might be asking yourself, *How do I know if he* can *change?* Perhaps on some level you do know, but the truth might be too frightening and the process of seeking solutions might seem too daunting. So here is a paint-by-number guide to facing your deal breaker.

WEIGH THE CONSEQUENCES. Ask yourself, *How bad is it? Is his problem tolerable or intolerable? If he refuses to change, can I live with it for the rest of my life?* Think carefully before you answer.

Does he make your high come down? How much? What is the emotional cost of being in this relationship? That on a normal day your mood ranges from "bad" to "not so bad"? That you fall asleep wondering, *If I enroll my children in therapy now, how long till they're healed?*

CONFRONT THE CONFUSION. What is your deal breaker? Is it that he won't make a commitment? That he is devaluing? That he only calls from restricted numbers and you do not know where he lives? That he refuses to break off his relationship with an old girlfriend? *Define it.*

In every relationship, there is a moment of clarity (usually after several minutes of eating chocolate chip cookies). The clouds part, and you see the situation for what it is. But if you tell yourself, *When we are alone, everything is magic; how could it be so bad?* or *Our chemistry is so great, I couldn't possibly live without him,* then it will be difficult to clearly confront problems in your relationship.

If you are attached to fantasy rather than reality, relate to bits and pieces rather than the whole picture, and continually settle for the appetizer rather than the whole meal, then your thinking will get cloudier and cloudier.

If you can't define your deal breaker, you will never broker your deal.

DO NOT BLAME YOURSELF. Perhaps you ask yourself, *What's wrong with me? Did I gain weight? Did I ask for too much? Was I too harsh? No, really—did I gain weight?* Own your own neuroses . . . but if you constantly blame yourself, you will never seek solutions and you will always feel confused. A deal breaker is a deal breaker is a deal breaker—and that's all there is to it!

Of course, you might irrationally hope that the problem is yours, because then it would be easier to fix. After all, holding your tongue, suppressing your needs, and going on a diet are all courses of action that are under your own control. But taking inappropriate responsibility for problems that are his, and only his, lets him off the hook and prolongs your misery.

On the other hand, if he only slightly fits the deal-breaking personality styles that I have outlined, yet you are unhappy, then you should reread this book with an eye to your own personality and begin to look inward rather than outward.

MAKE A PLAN. You have cleared the confusion and placed the responsibility upon him to fix his own problems. Now you must make a plan and set a time limit. Ask yourself: What am I going to do if he doesn't change? And how long am I willing to wait?

TAKE A STAND. Define your deal breaker for him. Give him three concrete examples of what is not working and tell him about your pain. If he interrupts, or says, "But you . . . ," explain to him that you will listen to his concerns *after* he has heard yours. If he explodes or walks out of the room, it is a deal breaker. If he hears you out, you must hear him out, and try to understand his feelings.

LET HIM COME UP WITH HIS OWN SOLUTIONS. This is the point at which you ask, "What is your intention toward this relationship? What plan are you going to devise to make this situation better?"

Do not nag or pressure. *And do not attempt to fix the problem on your own.* If he wants to change, he will. If he doesn't want to change, he won't. He is not deaf, dumb, or blind. And most certainly, he has listened to what you said. If he wants to work on it, you will observe signs of steady improvement. And if he doesn't want to work on it, it is a deal breaker and your relationship will never be transformed into what you need.

Remember: For every problem, there is a solution. And if he doesn't reach for his own solutions, you can still reach for yours.

(AND THIS IS HOW THE STORY GOES)

This is a story with two very different endings. In the first version, Jessica meets a young man with whom she wants to spend the rest of her life. They date for five years and eventually get engaged. Jessica knows that she wants to stay home for the first two years of her future children's lives. But her fiancé is a music teacher who only works a few days a week and never has enough money to pay his bills. Jessica is disturbed, but remains cloudy about the issue and never brings it to his attention.

On the eve of her wedding, Jessica considers asking him if he intends to work harder and make more money. But she becomes worried that she will alienate him and sour the nuptials. So Jessica gets married and hopes for the best.

Jessica is still waiting for her husband to get a steady job.

In the same story, but with a different ending, Jessica goes to therapy before she gets married and discusses the problem with her therapist. She realizes that she has never considered the negative impact of having a husband who does not fulfill his potential. Nor has she allowed herself to be clear about his aversion to work. She realizes that he has had plenty of professional opportunities but has failed to follow up on them. So she lets him know that if he is not willing to work full time, and if he cannot set a little money aside for their future, she cannot consider marriage. To her delight, he responds because he now knows what her deal breaker is. And because he loves her, he decides to confront his personal obstacles rather than lose the relationship.

Though the process of change is difficult, he seeks his own solutions instead of placing the burden on her.

Now . . . when you read the first version of the story, did you know where Jessica went wrong? And did you know what she should have done to fix her relationship problem? Were you aware that when she failed to clarify the problem, failed to set a time limit, and failed to ask for change, she was failing to face her deal breaker?

If you could not see where Jessica went wrong, you should seek internal clarity by rereading this book, talking to wise friends, finding a mentor, seeking therapy, and/or doing a little self-exploration.

If you *did* know the solution to Jessica's problem, and if you *did* know how she got derailed, then you know how to face a deal breaker.

Getting Off the Merry-Go-Round

Congratulations. Now you know how to face a deal breaker. But what happens when he promises to change, yet nothing improves at the level you need? You confront his excessive drinking and he cuts down temporarily, but never gets sober and refuses to go to a twelve-step meeting? And within six months he's drinking as much as before? Or you ask him to spend time with you, and he plans a romantic weekend but spends the next four days partying with his friends? How do you get off the merry-go-round?

CHAPTER 10

[Suzy's story]

Suzy came to therapy because she was unsure about how to proceed with her relationship. She had been with her boyfriend for five years, and they had two little boys together. But though she constantly asked for a commitment, he refused to move in or get married and she was still living with her mother. Recently Suzy's boyfriend had gone on a solo trip to Jamaica. While unpacking his suitcase, Suzy discovered a pair of women's underwear (red thong, size small). She panicked and called her girlfriends—but then irrationally told herself that the panties had probably fallen into his luggage by mistake.

Suzy frequently talked to her girlfriends about her relationship problems. But she obsessed about the details and paid no attention to her friends' opinions. When she finally took it to the next level by seeking professional psychological help, she began to glean insight into her own fear of seeking appropriate solutions.

[Alicia's story]

Alicia brought Ruben to therapy because she felt resentful and defeated. Whenever they were together, he demanded her full attention. For instance, he would talk to her while she was in another room, thus forcing her to leave what she was doing. But when she acted annoyed, he would accuse her of being defensive instead of linking her reaction to how he was treating her. When she tried to discuss the problem, he would agree to work on it. But the very next day, he would once again act like there was an invisible intercom between the two of them.

Ruben's overdependence was reflected in other areas, as he would emotionally withdraw whenever she did not cater to him or guess what he was thinking. He attended every therapy session and appeared to reflect upon the problem. But months passed, and his behavior did not substantially change.

Suzy and Alicia were both in relationships with deal breakers. In Suzy's relationship, the deal breaker was clear and the warning signs were obvious. In Alicia's relationship, the waters were muddy and the breaking point was unclear.

Suzy's boyfriend had never promised her anything. Alicia's man, on the other hand, held out the promise of a deal. But when it came to following through, he continually reneged, yet created the illusion that he was holding to his promise.

Has this happened to you? You confront the problem, but he still does not change? Or you ask him for something important, such as marriage or fidelity—but he minimizes your need? Or he continually makes promises but never follows through?

This is the stage at which confusion can set in. The stage at which you might be tempted to say:

"Am I overreacting?" (No.)

"But our relationship is so good when we don't fight." (Everyone's is.)

"Perhaps I should give him more time." (*More* time?)

"But he looks so good on paper." (So does "Lose Five Pounds in 10 Days!")

And though you read the last chapter, and though you know what to do, the lines keep getting blurrier and blurrier. You feel like you are on the edge of making it, but the answer never comes. You know what the problem is but are too afraid to think about it.

The merry-go-round syndrome sets in when he wants one thing and you want another—when he is unwilling to change and you are unwilling to confront the reality of what is happening in your relationship.

So why are you still on this merry-go-round? Perhaps you are afraid to strike out on your own and create the life that you want. Perhaps you are living out a script that was set for you early in life. Perhaps you have re-created the problems of your childhood and are hoping that this time you can be effective enough to change them. Perhaps you have found someone who feels familiar yet embodies a parent who was depriving or abusive. Perhaps you have become accustomed to worrying about his problems without expecting him to change.

Wake up, girlfriend! What's so bad about facing problems or drawing a line in the sand? Are you afraid of losing him? That your parents or clergy would be angry with you? That he would fall apart?

Does it feel unthinkable that the problem might not be solved? Or that you might have to let go of something that is not working in order to reach for something that is better?

Loss can be negotiated and reputations can be repaired. But a life can never be relived—so make sure that you are living it with the right person.

(SURE SIGNS THAT YOU ARE ON A MERRY-GO-ROUND)

You may not feel that you are on a merry-go-round. But if you worry about the relationship, yet nothing ever changes— you *are* on a merry-go-round. Here are the eleven most obvious signs:

1. You confront him about the problem. He seems to hear you and begins to alter his behavior. But two or three weeks pass, and you find yourself seething over the same thing that you asked him to change.

2. You feel confused. No matter how many times you talk about the topic, you never gain a clear understanding of the larger picture. And though you think you know what

he is talking about, you walk away from each discussion feeling more confused. Although he has created an alternate reality in which you want to believe (for instance, that he will propose marriage), the reality of the situation tells a different story (he never talks about the future and does not take you shopping for a ring).

3. Your life is racing by, and you keep waiting for things to get better. On important occasions, such as anniversaries and birthdays, you are reminded that nothing has changed.

4. You are more concerned about the future than the present, because the future seems hopeful and the present is miserable. You hate thinking about the present, because it forces you to make a decision.

5. You are more committed to his potential than to the reality of who he is. For instance, you think about what a great father he would be—even though he is a drug addict or he tells you that he does not want children.

6. Although he is willing to talk about the problem, he prefers things the way they are. For instance, he is willing to discuss the possibility of moving in together but insists that he would rather live on his own.

7. Although he claims to want to change, he is caught in the grip of an addiction for which he has not (or will not) seek treatment.

8. Because you keep fighting the same fight without alteration or change, you are eventually pushed into reactions that are not in keeping with your true nature. For instance, you scream at him during a fight although you have never sunk to that frightening depth before. Or you think about hiring a private detective, when all of your past relationships have been built upon trust.

9. You repeatedly fight over "nothing," but he refuses to seek help to find out what that "nothing" is.

10. He appears to reach for solutions, but they are all the wrong solutions. For instance, he agrees to make plans—but plans for something different from what you want. All his solutions are somewhat off target or slightly amiss. Although his gestures appear solid, they are never fully converted into giving you the things that you need.

11. He thinks you laugh too loud. You think he breathes too much.

[Karen's story]

Karen came to therapy because her boyfriend would not spend time alone with her. He was always with his buddies, at the beach, at tailgate parties, riding his motorcycle, or hanging out. This made her feel that *his* life was more important than *their* life. At her request, he came to therapy, and he appeared interested in my suggestions. Yet all his attempts to make the relationship better were slightly amiss. For instance, when I suggested that he check with Karen before making plans for the weekend, he complied. One weekend they made a plan to meet for dinner and go dancing. But when they arrived at the club, all his friends were there. Karen felt diminished and her hopes for an intimate evening were dashed.

Upon hearing the story, I commented to him, "But I suggested that you check in with Karen before making plans." He responded, "I did! Is it my fault that my friends decided to show up?"

I had the impression that if I asked him to knit a sweater, he would knit a sweater—but the wrong sweater. Or a sweater with three arms and two necks. He appeared to be trying, yet never got it right. And he would purposely fail, but then throw up his hands and act as though he felt pushed around. He led Karen to believe that he wanted to work on the relationship, but nothing progressed and nothing came to fruition.

Karen was on a merry-go-round.

When you are on a merry-go-round, you are always spinning, yet going nowhere. When you are on track, there is a sense of direction, movement, and progress. Karen's boyfriend did not value the relationship enough to make the changes that were needed. So Karen spun in circles and kept finding herself right back where she had started.

The only way to get off a merry-go-round is to stop the ride, step away, and walk in a different direction. Getting off the merry-go-round may be risky because he may not want to come along on your journey. But your life will not change if you are unwilling to change course.

Of course, if you are in a relationship with a serious problem, there is a possibility that he does want to change but has not been given the tools, time, or awareness. Or that the relationship *can* improve, but you simply have not found the right formula.

How do you know? If he wants a better relationship, he will be willing and sincere. The relationship will steadily improve, because he has joined forces with you in making it better. In the end, you will feel confident that he is following through.

Making a Deal

What happens when he *does* want to make it better? You've been talking to your friends about your relationship woes, but when you finally talk to him about your deal breaker, he says, "But, babe, I *do* want to want to be with you. Why are you so upset? I told you I wanted to work on it and that you are important to me." He reassures you, backs up his words through action, and demonstrates that he's willing to change even though he's let you down and there have been misunderstandings.

Now it's also up to you. There is movement, and you begin to feel hopeful but at the same time scared. Perhaps you even have a lightbulb moment, when you realize that both of you have been contributing to the problem.

It is time to ask yourself, *How am I contributing to this impasse? Is there something I need to learn about being a better girlfriend/wife? How do I rediscover the good part of him?*

This is how you 1) nurture a relationship while negotiating for what you want, and 2) learn to become the type of partner you also want him to be.

(RULE #1: LOVE YOURSELF)

Here's the deal: *Unless you feel like the prize, you will never find the courage to get what you want out of your relationship and your life.* If *he* is the prize, and you are nothing without him, you will find it difficult to confidently ask him to look at the issues that are bothering you. If *you* are the prize, however, it will feel inconceivable to remain in the relationship under miserable conditions.

When he—and only he—is the prize, you will feel jealous, anxious, insecure, and unable to negotiate for your needs. In your unending attempt to make him happy, you will feel reluctant to bring up insecurities or problems for fear of being discarded. Or, you will barrage him with your concerns but feel unable to break away if the situation does not resolve.

If, on the other hand, *you* are the prize, you will be able to call him out without fear of being retaliated against or abandoned! Because you are confident in your value, you will ask for what you need, because you will feel like a worthwhile investment. You will understand that the moment you ask him to appropriately accommodate your needs is the moment that you discover whether he truly loves you. And because your esteem comes from within, not from him, you are willing to take the risk. You understand that you are a loved individual, and this fact will not change—even if he chooses to leave the relationship.

Although you might waver in your resolve to hold true to yourself, you know that all your eggs are not in his basket. You have family and friends who love you, and you can create your own life, regardless of what happens between you and him.

Because you are confident in your worth, and because you feel loved in the world in general, you understand that being single is not a catastrophe—even if you do not have a date for a party or your mother pressures you to reunite with him. Although you could be questioned or criticized if you leave, you know how to restabilize and recapture the feeling that you are a catch.

Because you feel self-assured and important, you have clarity about the relationship problem that has turned into a deal breaker. You have given yourself permission to think about it, to talk to your family and friends, and you know your own mind. Thus, you are able to clearly outline the course of events that have deteriorated your happiness in this relationship.

You feel that you have a voice and do not have to be passive, controlling, or demanding. You confidently reveal your thoughts and give him a chance to respond.

(RULE #2: LEARN TO LOVE HIM)

When he agrees to change, it is probably because something in *you* has changed. Once you begin to place value on yourself, you can learn to place value on him. And once you learn to love yourself, you can believe that *he* places value on *you* and is motivated to change. Because you have become a more secure person, you trust that he is sincere, and you give him new opportunities to become the man you need him to be.

When you discover your value and he begins to respond, it is time to work on the problem. But how do you help the man who wants to help himself? How do you nurture and encourage him? How do you make your garden grow?

HAVE YOUR OWN LIFE. Regardless of what is happening in the relationship, go forward with your day. Honor yourself and make your own plans. If he does not call, go out. If he does not change, move on with your life.

HAVE REGULAR CONVERSATIONS ABOUT THE RELATION-SHIP. Every solution begins with a dialogue. Talk to him about your needs and feelings. And encourage him to express himself to you.

FIND WAYS TO GET YOUR MESSAGE ACROSS. If you have told him what you need but he still does not hear you, say it in a different way. Perhaps you need to write it down. Perhaps you need to use language that he can understand. Perhaps you need to bring in a third party who can explain it to him (interpretive dance?). The problem may be clear to you but not to him. Be flexible, and take into account his personality and his differences. Keep in mind his personality type and use it as a guide.

DO NOT GRIND. Do not obsess, and do not repeat the same thing over and over again. If he tells you that he has heard you, trust him. Fixating on your explanations will alienate him and cause him to withdraw.

ACCEPT HIM. Ask yourself, What drew me to this man? This is the man you have chosen; this is the man you love. Accept him for who he is rather than who you hoped he would be—because if you don't like him, there is no deal!

Men have their own personalities and their own skill set (like hanging a picture or making the toilet stop running). And this is what attracted you in the first place, so get used to it!

TRY TO UNDERSTAND HIS POINT OF VIEW. Put yourself in his shoes and try to see the situation through his eyes, even if you don't want to. Listen to what he *is* saying rather than what you *think* he is saying. Do not become offended and do not be disturbed at what he is trying to tell you.

SHOW APPRECIATION. Ask yourself, *When he makes the changes I want, will I be appreciative, happy, and satisfied? Or do I need to be unhappy in order to be in this relationship?* If you cannot be satisfied, then either 1) you need to be unhappy in order to avoid intimacy and you should work on your own problems, or 2) he is not the right man and you should set him free.

INVEST IN THE RELATIONSHIP. A relationship is like a bank account. The more you invest, the more it grows. So spend time together, have sex, do special favors, and prioritize each other.

Ask him, "What makes you happy? What turns you on?" Nurture him according to his needs as well as yours. Just because a day at the spa or a deep discussion is a bonding experience for you, it may not necessarily be a bonding experience for him. Find out what he wants, and be sure to mutually accommodate each other.

SEEK HELP FOR SERIOUS PROBLEMS. If he suffers from a severe problem, such as substance abuse, sex or pornography addiction, online affairs, or mental illness, then he needs to seek rehab, medical help, therapy, or a twelve-step program. These problems are his, and his alone. And he must seek his own solutions. Your job is to offer appropriate support as he helps himself.

Everybody has emotional needs. For most, these needs include feelings of security, love, and trust. He is no different from you. He needs to feel that you are there for him and are interested in being in the relationship. If you enter the relationship and then refuse to nurture or appreciate him, he will not respond. And if you invest only according to what is important to you, then you will end up with someone who is empty or masochistic.

If he wants to work with you, and you want to be with him, then you must find out what he wants and make an effort too.

[Rachael's story]

Rachael met Travis soon after a heart-wrenching breakup. Just as she was about to give up hope of ever finding another man, Travis came into her life. After a year of dating, they moved in together. Because Travis had been attentive while they were dating, Rachael anticipated that he would devote himself to the relationship. But guess what? Three months after signing the lease and decorating their condo, Travis began to drift away. Rachael would ask him to e-mail a "save the date" for an impending party, but he could not be bothered to take the time. And Rachael would ask Travis to assist her in cleaning the house, but he seemed uninterested. Small requests turned into battles, and Rachael began to feel frustrated and angry.

At the beginning, both of them brought their best selves to the relationship. And Rachael had hoped that if she held out her hand, he would take it. But now she found herself holding her own hand. The veil had been lifted, familiarity had set in, and his true personality was revealed.

So Rachael decided to go away for the weekend with a few good friends. While apart, she thought about the problem and clarified her thoughts. She also put on a sexy dress, went out with her friends for sushi and martinis, and was reminded that she was still a hot commodity.

Because Rachael had given herself time, space, and objectivity, she was able to approach the problem from a whole new perspective. She told Travis that she was becoming more aware of her frustration and what she needed from the relationship. She also let him know that his lack of responsiveness was eroding her good will. She let him know that if he could take her hand, and could join forces in making the relationship better, she would remain dedicated. If he could not, she would have to leave.

Instead of remaining resentful, Rachael took responsibility for her own life and paved the way for Travis to respond. Because Rachael was able to love herself, Travis began to see her in a new light and recognize her importance. He was able to transition from resistance to mutuality, respect, and willingness to work on the relationship. And as he began to change, Rachael remained mindful of their differences. She realized that Travis did not like big parties and house-cleaning on demand, so she tailored her expectations to take into account his true personality. As Travis changed, Rachael recommitted herself to the relationship.

What Rachael and Travis learned is that a relationship is like a garden. It either grows or it withers. And if it is not tended to, it does not thrive. Once it withers past a certain point, no amount of water or sunshine can revive it.

Negotiating a Deal CHAPTER 12

He wants a better relationship, and you believe him! You feel good about yourself and you feel good about him, too. But his problems are still there, even though he is working on them. And you worry about whether he'll be able to offer you the happiness that you deserve. You keep asking yourself, *How do I make this relationship better?*

For instance, he promises to spend more time with the children, but arrives at their soccer games halfway through and then leaves before congratulating them on their sportsmanship. Or he makes a devaluing comment in front of your friends, such as "Are you going to wear *that* tonight?" —even though he promised that he would treat you better. And when you remind him of his promise to change, he observes that he has relapsed. Nonetheless, his issues remain and he can't seem to get a handle on them.

You want to keep working on it and take the relationship to the next level. But you have also begun to realize that the relationship needs more help.

[Lisa's story]

When Lisa first met Steve, he appeared easygoing. But within a few months he began to interject his advice. If Lisa said, "I am going to the store," Steve would say, "Don't forget to take your wallet!" And if she brought home a can of tuna, he would question, "Haven't you read about the mercury levels in the ocean?" If she switched from tuna to steak, he would comment, "Perhaps you should go easy on the high-fat food." Steve's interjections undermined Lisa's judgment and derailed her from thinking independently.

At about the sixth month, the relationship imploded. Lisa told Steve that she was tired of being treated like a child. And though Steve could concede that he was overbearing, and though he genuinely wanted to change, he had difficulty distinguishing between right and being controlling.

Steve needed help.

*   *   *

When Lisa came to therapy, I helped her understand that Steve was a Man in Charge. As she began to decipher his personality type, she began to pinpoint their underlying relationship conflicts. She formulated a plan, moved forward in an informed manner, and began to communicate in a way that made sense to both of them. Comprehending his personality helped her know what to expect, how to make the relationship as successful as possible, and how to gauge their progress.

When you were reading about the five deal-breaking personality types, what personality type did your man fit into? Each type benefits from a separate approach; thus, I'm going to reveal a strategy tailor-made for your man.

(HOW TO NEGOTIATE A DEAL IF HE'S A SCRIPTWRITER)

If he's a Scriptwriter, he probably confuses his *fantasies* about who you are with the *reality* of who you are, and his personal history with your present-day relationship. For instance, if he wants a commitment, he will probably imagine that you want one too! He might even imagine that you have a ring on your finger. If he is hungry, he might experience you as hungry and then coerce you into eating. If he was raised by a mother who was needy, he may envision you as needy. But the more he sees his face in your face, and the more he projects onto you his own wishes, fears, and longings, the more alienated and misunderstood you will feel.

The best way to work on a relationship with a Scriptwriter is to let him know that he is not seeing you clearly and then to write your own role—no matter what he says. For instance, if he has cast you in the role of betrayer and you refrain from going out with your friends in order to avoid his wrath or anxiety—stop it! Go out! Live your own life!

If he has cast you in the role of princess and treats you like a delicate flower even though you are quite capable, fight the typecasting! Act like the sturdy person you know you are, and do not let yourself become immobilized or helpless.

Remember that The Scriptwriter turns feelings into facts and fears into realities. It can be difficult to extricate yourself from a role once he has cast you in it—so get his cooperation and understanding before writing your own scenario. Explain to him that he does not see you clearly. Outline for him the differences between his ideas about you and who you know you are. Warn him that you have been suppressing your true personality in order to fulfill his expectations and that he should expect different behavior from you in the future.

If he can take in new information about you, both of you can grow. If he is completely unwilling to rewrite the script, there is nothing you will be able to do. You will either live the rest of your life in his reality or have plenty of fights ahead.

(HOW TO NEGOTIATE A DEAL IF HE'S A MAN IN CHARGE)

If he's a Man in Charge, he will resist your independence and question your decisions. And when you exercise your own judgment or ask for privacy, he might take corrective measures. For instance, if you ask him to refrain from looking at your BlackBerry, he will ask, "What do you have to hide?" And if you tell him that you have nothing to hide, he will say, "Then why are you keeping secrets?" He will make you feel guilty, and thus will have power over you.

A good way to redirect your relationship with this man is to select one area into which he continually intrudes against your will. Explain to him that you have read this insightful book (perhaps he should read it too), and have decided to set a few boundaries. For instance, you could tell him not to expect a phone call during your business day unless it's at a time that works for you. Or you could tell him that you want to go shopping without repercussions. Or you could ask him to refrain from interrupting your conversation the next time you are on the phone. If he can respect your boundaries and begin to control his anxieties instead of controlling you, then the relationship is workable. If he distorts your good intention of making things better, then why would you want to continue?

(HOW TO NEGOTIATE A DEAL IF HE'S A MAN WITHOUT FAULT)

The Man Without Fault already feels that he has all the right answers. In mild cases he will refuse to open himself to discussion or disagreement. In more severe cases he will feel that he is "the way, the truth, and the light." This man believes that if only you had listened to him, you would have known what to do. In his mind, he is morally superior. He is the high priest, and the world is his flock—even if he has no true accomplishments and nothing to show for himself.

The Man Without Fault comes in many packages. He might be the holder of what is right in the world, or the one who is frustrated with the stupidity of everyday life.

The best way to work on a relationship with The Man Without Fault is to pull aside the veil and ask yourself, *Who is this man, really? Is he everything he has held himself out to be? Do I really need to feel inferior or afraid?* Like the little boy in "The Emperor's New Clothes," you must look beyond this man's showiness and self-promotion and question everything that he has told you about himself.

If you decide to stay in a relationship with this man, it is important to count the cost. Even if he works on the relationship, he will be tempted to diminish you for the rest of your life (like celebrating *your* promotion with *his* new Lexus). So before moving forward, do a cost-benefit analysis. What do you get out of this relationship? Does the good outweigh the bad?

The next step is to let him know that you are going to call him on his devaluing and hurtful comments and expect him to empathize. Since The Man Without Fault finds it almost impossible to put himself in your shoes, you must tell him how you feel when he devalues you. You might say, "When you said _____, I felt _____," or "Your comment hurt me." If things get rocky, seek professional help, as it might become impossible to go it alone.

Because The Man Without Fault is concerned primarily with himself, you have probably abandoned personal goals and then stood by while he gives others the praise and compliments that you deserve. The next step is to tell him that you are going to begin reaching for your own goals and asking for more appreciation.

Warning: The Man Without Fault will happily support you in endeavors that reflect favorably upon him. For instance, he may purchase a breast augmentation if he feels you would look better on his arm. He may encourage you to go to college if he feels that he would look more important with a wife or girlfriend with a degree. But once you blossom on your own, he could feel resentful, cheated, and undermined by your success.

If The Man Without Fault supports you in a reasonable venture that has nothing to do with him, you might be able to work on it. If he cannot support you in an activity that is important only to you, then your life with him will be limited and compromised.

(HOW TO NEGOTIATE A DEAL IF HE'S AN INVISIBLE MAN)

The Invisible Man keeps disappearing and disappearing. And when you summon him, he reappears—only to disappear again!

It can be deceiving to work on a relationship with this man because he *appears* to attach, but in reality attaches to all the wrong things. And it is difficult to complain, because he is spending hours cleaning the garage, loading programs onto your computer, coaching Little League, walking the dog, et cetera. He is always doing, yet never connecting.

The best way to work on a relationship with this man

is to help him see that making a connection will enliven the relationship and enrich both your lives. If he does not understand the benefit of making a deeper connection, then the relationship will remain empty and unfulfilling.

Note: A lot of men become invisible when they no longer want to be in a relationship. Do not delude yourself into thinking that he is overwhelmed by intimacy when in fact he does not want to be with you!

If he tells you (without coercion) that he really wants this relationship, then he must try to acknowledge your importance in tangible and meaningful ways. For instance, if he spends the entire day working on your computer, he should break away for lunch together. Or finish in time to go to dinner and a movie.

If he resists intimacy because he feels controlled by everybody, or because it is safer to bet on a sports game than to bet on a relationship, or easier to perfect his body through exercise than to perfect his communication shills, then he needs to take hold of his fears and risk spending quality time with you.

If it is a workable situation, one good experience will build upon another and the relationship will get better. But if you are pushing and he is pulling, and if the relationship feels like an ongoing struggle, then you should examine your need to be in a relationship that is depriving for you and oppressive for him.

(HOW TO NEGOTIATE A DEAL IF HE'S A LITTLE BOY WHO POSES AS A MAN)

The Little Boy Who Poses as a Man will charm his way into your life and into your heart, because he is unconflicted and carefree. *You* may worry about paying the bills, but he is unconcerned (however, he does have a credit card that gives reward points at Chuck E. Cheese). *You* may worry about what the host of the party thinks when you leave early, but he feels that everything is fine. *You* may think about tomorrow, but he is filled with thoughts of today.

This is charming—for now. But once you spend time together, when familiarity has set in and he is feeling comfy, he will lapse into a little boy who wants to be taken care of. And what are you going to do then? What happens when you do all the work, and he goes out and plays? What happens when you are honored at an awards banquet, and he becomes needy or demanding? What happens when you meet your potential, but he never meets his? What happens when he expects you to take care of him and begins to take you for granted?

Here's what you do. Explain to him that he needs to grow up because you do not want to spend your life with a child. Then let him know that at the first hint that he cannot regulate his feelings and impulses (he gets jealous, loses his temper, or gets drunk) or the first glimpse that he is slipping (he forgets to pay a bill or has an affair without considering the devastating consequences), you are going to either leave the relationship or refuse to clean up his mess! That is what you are going to do!

If he misses a bill, do not pay it (but if his irresponsibility is affecting your credit, first separate your finances). If he becomes jealous, do not cater to his fears. If he develops a substance abuse problem, do not locate a rehab hospital or attempt to get him to a twelve-step meeting. If he cannot find a job, do not subsidize his living. Do not act like his mother, and *do not* do his work for him.

What would you do if he were a real little boy? If you were a good mother, you would let him fall and make his own mistakes, and expect him to learn and grow.

If you can grow him up instead of growing him down, if you can hold him to the same standards to which other adults adhere, if you can support him in his growth rather than taking responsibility for his shortcomings, then you can in good conscience know if he is the right partner and whether the relationship will work. If he does not grow, and if you continue to "mother," you enable him. And will that really bring you happiness?

(CLOSING THE DEAL)

When you successfully negotiate a relationship deal, you show your hand and reveal yourself, instead of holding your feelings close to the vest. This gives both of you an opportunity to negotiate for what you want. When you reveal yourself, you give him a chance to respond. When he begins to respond, you must respond to him, too.

Are you keeping your unhappiness a secret and holding it deep inside because you are reluctant to discover whether he cares? Or whether he is motivated to work on the relationship? Perhaps you have a storehouse of memories. Or a joint mortgage. Or more important, children. And you want to give the relationship your best effort.

If you communicate your needs, he may disappoint you. And yes, you may have to leave and break up a situation that is miserable yet familiar. But this is the risk you must take in order to initiate a process of mutual exploration and potentially make the relationship better.

Breaking the Deal   CHAPTER 13

You've tried everything. You've laid yourself bare and given him a chance to respond. But your efforts have gone nowhere and your good intentions have yielded no results. For instance, you clarified the issue and repeatedly told him how you felt, yet the problems continued and he made no attempt to work on them. As you reflect, you realize that his failure to respond is, in and of itself, the true deal breaker. And as much as you hate to admit it, it is time to vote yourself off the island.

Has this happened to you? You've made a good-faith effort, but the relationship has stalled and your balancing act is tilting out of control? Would you like to know how to break the deal?

[Lauren's story]

Lauren met Cal while they were in college. After dating for a year, they decided that they would both finish school and then get married. Lauren made it clear that she eventually wanted to start a family, and Cal agreed.

After graduating from college, they moved in together. But Cal went on to medical school without proposing marriage! For years Lauren waited. After obtaining his medical degree, Cal established a successful practice as an orthopedic surgeon. When Lauren inquired again about marriage, he suggested that they first build their dream home together. So Lauren met with an architect, worked with the decorator, and helped him build his dream home. Meanwhile, Cal cruised around town in the silver Porsche that he had bought for himself. One day Lauren broke down and revealed to Cal that she was growing more and more despondent about their future. She had the house, the boyfriend, and the life. However, his future looked bright and hers was growing dim because there was no sign of marriage or children.

Upon reflection Lauren realized that she had tried everything. Yet when she gave Cal an ultimatum, he begged for more time. And so another year passed, but there was still no sign that he was working on the problem. Lauren began to notice that he had not expressed any particular conflicts or fears regarding marriage. He simply did not want a commitment.

Once Lauren defined her deal breaker—that she was a lover rather than a wife and that the relationship was at an impasse—she began to think about other things that were wrong with their relationship. She began to notice that they were always feathering his nest but never building a future together. And that no matter what she said, there was never an adequate explanation as to why they were not getting married.

Is Lauren's story your story? You want one thing and he wants another? You want to work on the relationship and he doesn't? You know that the relationship needs to change, but he feels that it is fine the way it is? You want to stay in the relationship but know that it is time to leave?

When a deal-breaking disagreement becomes the glue that holds a relationship together, when fighting is more important than a cure, when ugliness is a habitual way of being in a relationship, when empathy is rare, and when regrets and hindsight are more important than hopefulness and optimism, then any relationship problem—no matter how seemingly trivial or petty—is a true deal breaker, and a tragedy.

(HOW TO LEAVE THE ONE YOU LOVE)

BREAK THE RULES. Relationships, like games, are governed by very specific rules. Usually, these rules are established in the beginning and are very difficult to change. The unhealthier the relationship, the stricter the rules will be. For example, he may have established a rule that you should never disagree with him. Or that you should not express your feelings freely. Or that you should be there for him, no matter what he does. Or that you should stand by while he endlessly attends sports games, goes drinking, plays golf, et cetera.

In order to break the deal, you have to be willing to retract your agreements. For instance, you may have to make it clear that you will no longer tie up your future without a commitment—though you appeared to agree to this arrangement in the past. Or you may have to make it clear that you will no longer pay his bills—though there has been an unconscious agreement that you will pick up the pieces whenever his life is falling apart. Or you may have to break your implicit agreement to stand by while he flirts with other girls—though you have stood by repeatedly. If you want to break the deal, you have to break the rules. And if you want to break the rules, you must stand firm in your resolve.

FACE YOUR FEARS. Ask yourself, *What is holding me in this relationship? Why am I afraid to leave?*

Are you terrified of being alone? That you will never find another person to love? That no one will love you like he does (even though he has made little attempt to meet your needs)? That something is better than nothing? That the devil you know is better than the devil you don't know? That your life will be compromised after losing your mutual friends, your home, your lifestyle, and the opportunities that have come your way because of him?

Relationships are hard to give up because they give you an identity and a sense of self-esteem (they also provide you with a date for weddings and a ride to the airport). Relationships make you feel desirable and give you the assurance that you are loved. When you are in a relationship, you feel that someone is there for you.

Leaving a relationship can feel frightening and difficult. But loss is not a catastrophe, and the end of a relationship is not the end of the world. And even though you may feel sad, you *do* have the capacity to recover. Because when you face your fears, you pave the way for a life that is more fulfilling and rewarding.

MAKE A PLAN. If you have children, think carefully about how you are going to help them adjust to the loss. If you are in an abusive relationship, and they are older, they might be relieved at the thought that you are finally going to leave (countless times, in clinical practice, adult patients have confided in me that throughout childhood they yearned for a parent to leave an abusive partner). Regardless of your circumstances, however, you will need to make a careful plan. Meet with a therapist. Plan what you are going to say to your children. And reassure them that this separation is not their fault and that they are loved by both of you. Then tell them that you and your partner's guilt only means *more* presents for them at the holidays and an opportunity to blame *you* for *their* future relationship shortcomings!

What children need most are two parents who love each other—even if they have separated. If you have decided to leave, shore up your friendship with your ex as much as possible (or at the very least, make agreements to say only nice things about each other) so that your children can feel secure.

GATHER A SUPPORT NETWORK. Before leaving your relationship, line up friends and family for support. This might be difficult if you have tried unsuccessfully to break off the relationship many times before. But assure them that this time it is different, and this time you need their full support. A girls' night out, a sleepover with a friend and a good bottle of wine, gossiping with a group of friends whom you once enjoyed but have fallen out of touch with—all are good therapy and all will buffer you through the difficult times ahead!

PRACTICE THE BREAKUP SPEECH. The breakup speech goes something like this: "This relationship is no longer working for me. I have tried everything possible to make it better [back this up with a few examples] and I have asked you to follow through with some important things that I need [back this up with a few examples]. But you have failed to follow through, so I'm done and it's over."

Do not be surprised if he tries to dissuade you or comes knocking at your door. Just because the relationship was not-so-good for you does not necessarily mean that it wasn't working for him. And though he may not have wanted to improve the relationship, he probably enjoyed having you in his life.

If he refuses to separate, or does not take no for an answer, say, "Do not call, e-mail, text-message, or otherwise contact me." If he is an overgrown child or a stalker type, anything other than "You may not contact me" will be considered an invitation to reengage, and he will continue to call.

Once you have broken up, resolve your neurotic guilt. Guilt is a feeling that you have done something wrong. But what is wrong about leaving something that is not working and reaching for the life that you want?

Remember: Although he was in a relationship with you, he does not own you.

THE AGONY OF SELF-DECEIT. Once you leave, you may be tempted to question yourself: *Should I have left? What if he is the best man out there? Maybe I was the bitch. What if I hadn't said those mean things? Then he wouldn't have acted that way and I wouldn't have had to leave.*

But, ladies—the reality is, he made your life miserable. And no, he's not the best man out there. If he had been, you wouldn't have needed to leave him.

LEARN TO GRIEVE. Grieving is remembering for the sake of forgetting. By this, I mean that when you grieve you think about your boyfriend/husband and everything that you did together. You tell and retell your story, to yourself and to your friends. And as you remember, and as you linger over the memories, they will eventually be given up and no longer hold the meaning that they did in the past.

When you grieve, you long for your man, and the world temporarily feels like an empty place. You lose your appetite, feel uninterested in going out and spending time with your friends, and freak out when they offer to set you up with someone new. But if you can reach out to others and instill your life with meaning—even if you don't want to—you will begin to feel that you have something to hold on to. So go to a movie, spend time with your friends, tell your story, and do everything possible to create a sense that your life is meaningful and full.

MEMORIZE THE GRIEVING MANTRA. Tell yourself, *Why would I want someone who cannot love me as I deserve to be loved?* Repeat this mantra until you are finished grieving (only not out loud and in public—people will stare). It is important because it will help you accept the truth and move on. Beware: Blaming yourself will only make you feel guilty and depressed. Recognizing his inability to love you will mobilize a grieving process and help you separate from him and eventually love again.

CREATE A GRIEVING RITUAL. When you are ready, create a grieving ritual. This is an action that you take in order to get him out of your mind. Perhaps you ceremoniously delete his number from your cell phone. Or you get a few of his belongings that he has left behind, put them in a box, insert a picture that was meaningful, set the box on fire, and watch as the past goes up in smoke. If you are tempted to hold on to his number or to dive in and retrieve the belongings before they disappear, you are not truly relinquishing the relationship. Remind yourself of why you left and keep repeating the grieving mantra until you are ready to let go.

Grieving is disillusionment. When you grieve, you give up your hopes and dreams of a future with that particular person.

If you cannot allow yourself to be disappointed, you will never grieve and move on. And if all you can think about are the things you wanted to do with him, then you will spin in circles rather than move forward with your life. Remember: You left him because the relationship was not working. And if you cannot let go of a relationship that is not working, you will never be able to reach for a relationship that is better.

Shopping List for a Healthy Man

By now you should have a firm grasp on recognizing and facing deal breakers. But sometimes you can do everything right yet *still* not get the result that you want. Let's say he stopped having sex with you. So you clarified the problem, talked and talked, and tried to understand the deeper issue. You also stepped back and let him assume responsibility for his part of the problem. Then you went out and bought expensive lingerie, but the only thing that rose was the balance on your credit cards.

Or you are with a man who stopped listening and calling, so you disappeared for a few days, hoping that he would notice, start calling, and return to the attentive way he was at the beginning of the relationship. But the only person who noticed anything amiss was you—when the call never came and he barely realized that you were missing (and you realized that it wasn't a deal breaker because there wasn't even a deal).

Perhaps you decided to take back your life. So you retrieved the mind that you lost when you were so busy agreeing with him. And you began to stand up to him and assert your point of view. But instead of feeling attracted to the new you who felt better about herself, he felt threatened, went on the attack, and reduced you to the size of a Chihuahua.

What are you going to do? Continue to feel crappy? Work harder than he's working to fix problems in the relationship? Leave, but then pick the same type of man over and over again?

Or are you going to find a good guy—the type of man who brings out the best you in the best possible way? It's not always what you do but who you *select* in the first place.

But do you know what a healthy man looks like? And if you found him, would you want him? Or would you run straight to the nearest bad boy, convincing yourself that he is the one who will make you happy?

When you can stop deluding yourself and begin to make better choices, you are ready to go shopping for a healthy man. This is what to look for:

When you first meet a man, whether it's online, at the grocery store, at a bar, at school, or at your job, you should feel that he wants you. It may be conveyed by a look, a touch, a compliment, curiosity, or attention to detail. And it must, within a short amount of time, be conveyed in person—not online, through a text message, or on the phone. And *definitely*, it should be backed up by his willingness to make a plan and move the relationship forward. If he's not interested enough to call in advance and make a plan, he's not interested enough to invest his emotions in a relationship. Conversely, constant calling, e-mailing, and text-messaging is not true contact. He cannot touch you, see you, adore you, or get to know you through words on a screen or over the phone.

Soon after meeting him, you should discover that he has appropriately achieved in at least one area of his life. For instance, if he went to college he now has a good job. Or a decent car. If he inherited his parents' business, he has learned how to successfully manage it. Or if he is a member of a baseball team, he has learned to become a team player. His efforts continue to generate new opportunities, new skills, new challenges, or new possessions. Thus, he is progressing and not degenerating.

If he's a healthy man, he will never make plans for the future that he does not intend to back up. And he will certainly not say, "I'm not sure where this relationship is going," and then continue to call you and have sex with you. He will not send messages that are confusing and difficult to decipher. *A healthy man says what he means and means what he says. And the words that he speaks are backed up by action that coincides.* Even if he cannot give a guarantee, the relationship is always moving forward. Thus, you will never find yourself drunk-dialing at two in the morning because you fear that he is out with another girl. Or find yourself in a situation where he claims to want to get married, but you are the only one who is planning the wedding and paying for the caterer.

If you are in the right relationship, it will feel reciprocal and mutual. When you offer emotional support, is he appreciative? Does he give back by surprising you with a special little something? Or remembering your favorite drink?

Do you feel that what he gives is as valuable and meaningful as what you offer? For instance, if you set aside a Saturday night, will he make an entertainment plan that is enjoyable for both of you? If your car breaks down, will he come and get you? If you have a problem, will he help you? Is he as devoted to you as you are to him?

Healthy relationships are based upon mutual give-and-take. And what is given and received should feel of equal value. If the only thing that you are getting out of this relationship is text messages or e-mails, occasional plans, or the assurance that you won't be alone on a Saturday night, you are not getting what you need.

If he's the right guy for you, he will have good friends and you will like who he is when he's with them. Whether he's at the bar, at a tailgate party, or running for political office, you are confident that he is the man you know and love, both with you or apart from you. When he's out of sight, he does not turn into somebody else. For instance, a player. Or a jerk. Conversely, when you include him with your friends, you know who he will be—charming and engaging, enhancing instead of detracting.

If he's a healthy man, he will like you for who you are. Even if you have a bad day or say something that he does not like, his adoration will remain steady and his view of you will remain the same. Beware of the guy whose perception changes whenever you deviate from his expectations. For instance, you dress a certain way and he refuses to hold you or compliment you. Or you gain weight and he stops having sex with you.

Does he take pleasure in you, whether you look sexy in your low-rider jeans or have just gotten out of bed? Does he spend time with your family because he knows that you are a part of them? Is he interested in your spirituality? Or do you feel that you must suppress your personality in order to hold on to his approval? Even when it comes to your sexual preferences, you should feel free to reveal yourself without fear of losing his affection.

A healthy man will never view you as unconditionally bad or make you feel terrible about yourself. Even in the midst of an argument, he will be able to see both the good and the bad in you. For instance, he will not stay mad at you once the argument is over. And he will move on instead of clinging to bad feelings or suspicions. He loves you and sees you as a good person, no matter what. And he would *never* refuse to call, refuse to be nice, or walk out the door without quickly returning—simply because you shared your concerns with him.

If he is the right guy, he will tolerate the unexpected and the unknown because he trusts you. For instance, he will not pin you down or put a leash on you every moment of the day in order to feel secure. Instead, he will respect your boundaries and give you the privacy and independence you deserve. Conversely, he will have his own private self without doing things that are hurtful to you, blocking you out, or using distance to keep the upper hand.

Because he has a good sense of himself and remains solid even when you are apart, your circle of friends and opportunities continue to expand and you do not need his permission to pursue your interests.

A healthy man has a learning curve. For instance, if you tell him that you need more time together or need him to stop doing something that is obnoxious, he will shift his behavior because he loves you and does not want to lose you. He is willing to learn from his mistakes and modify his actions. For instance, if he begins a friendship with a flirtatious girl and you let him know that this is creating a problem, he will be concerned about your feelings and come up with a solution.

When you discuss relationship obstacles, he works on them. He would never admit to a substance abuse problem and then refuse to address it. Or agree to appropriately separate from his mother (who dislikes you) but then go running back to the nest.

If he is healthy, he will seek his own solutions. For instance, if he has a problem he will reach out to others for help, find resources, have a conversation, go to therapy, attend a twelve-step program—anything that will move him closer to making the changes that he needs to make. (You could do worse than give him this book. No, wait—make him buy his own damn copy!) Petty pride, laziness, or stubbornness will not keep him from taking the steps that he needs to take to have a full relationship with you.

A healthy man will not try to have power over you. He won't leave you wondering where he is and what he is doing. Or leave you hanging just to prove a point. Or make you feel that you have to disappear for a few days to recover the power you once had.

Even if he has more money, status, and power, he will not make you feel that you would be nothing without him. A healthy man is willing to take you into account instead of pushing you away. He is willing to listen, meet your needs, and include you in mutual decision making. Because you matter, he does not want to have undue influence or control over you. And he can trust that he is loved, even when he is not in charge. When it comes to who takes care of whom, and who makes the decisions, and who gets the last say, he is willing to negotiate (because really, all of life is a little like *Let's Make a Deal*).

A healthy man feels grateful for what you offer. He acknowledges that you provide him with something that he cannot provide for himself. And he knows that you are a special person with your own gifts and talents. When he expresses gratitude, he acknowledges the goodness in you.

It is not a good sign when you find yourself giving and giving but he never says thank you or acknowledges what you have done for him. Or once in a while he throws you a crumb, but you are left with the feeling that he does not appreciate your contribution. Or you realize that he does not show appreciation or admiration because he is envious or resentful of your accomplishments.

If you continually find yourself in relationships that are not working, you should ask yourself, *Where am I going wrong?*

Am I re-creating my painful past in my current relationships? Am I refusing to be open to new experiences? Am I attracting the wrong guys because I am not the emotionally healthy person that I expect a man to be?

Perhaps you do not expect to be treated well. Or you fear being intimate with a man who wants you. Or you dread the confines of a commitment.

Perhaps *you* are a Scriptwriter, and believe that because your father cheated on your mother, and your last two boyfriends cheated on you, he will cheat on you too. So you fulfill your own self-defeating prophecy by unknowingly choosing cheaters. But your poor choices only fuel your disillusionment and unconsciously ensure that you will never have the relationship that you truly want.

So why don't you muster the courage to date a different sort of man—one you might not normally be attracted to, one who does not necessarily conform to your fantasy or ideal?

And why don't you choose a relationship that does not spontaneously combust, as all your other relationships have in the past? (If it does, it is a deal breaker, because your past relationships didn't work out, did they?) Just because he *doesn't* instantly turn you on or *doesn't* keep you up all night crying *doesn't* mean that he is not the one for you.

Whether you're shopping, looking, or have purchased, the real deal is inside you. It is the *you* that you take from relationship to relationship and from experience to experience (the *you* who knows your value, knows what you think and feel, and makes your own decisions). It is the series of choices that you make along the way. It is the larger picture that you hold in your mind. The picture of who he is and who you are when you are with him. It is knowing what you want and knowing that you will never make the same bad choice again. And that if you do, you are willing to stop yourself and start over again. It is the willingness to grow past your beginnings, take responsibility for new experiences, and create the love life that you want.

The real deal is knowing that happiness is a choice and that at the end of your life you will look back and say, "Every day I felt the way I wanted to feel about myself with this man."

About the Author

Bethany Marshall, PhD, PsyD, MFT has been in private practice as a marriage, family, and child therapist in both Beverly Hills and Pasadena for the past eighteen years. She regularly appears as a contributing psychological commentator on *Good Morning America*, *The Early Show*, and Leeza Gibbons's nationally syndicated radio show, "Hollywood Confidential," and is a weekly commentator for *Nancy Grace* on CNN Headline News. She lives in Southern California.